THE SOUTHERN COWBOY
COOKBOOK

THE SOUTHERN COWBOY
COOKBOOK

John Rivers

PHOTOGRAPHY BY
DIANA ZALUCKY

story farm

WINTER PARK • MIAMI • SANTA BARBARA

The Southern Cowboy Cookbook
Copyright © 2013 by John Rivers
www.4rsmokehouse.com

All rights reserved.
No portions of this book may be copied or distributed without express written permission of the author and Story Farm, LLC.

Published in the United States by Story Farm, LLC.
www.story-farm.com

Library of Congress Cataloging-in-Publication Data is available upon request.
ISBN 978-0-9839053-8-7
Printed in China

Editorial director: Ashley Fraxedas
Book design: Hatchet Design, www.hatchetdesign.com
   Art Director: Jason Farmand
   Designers: David Claytor, Morgan Claytor
Photo styling: Katie Farmand
Copy editors: Karen Cakebread, Ken Clarke, Eva Dougherty
Recipe development: John Rivers
Chief expediters: Jeff Palermo, John Hufferd
Culinary manager: Jenny Herbert
Head baker: Amanda Eubanks
Recipe testers: Pam Brandon, Katie Farmand, Jill Mross
Whipcracker: Sarah Hufferd
Creative assistants: Cassie Shriner, Melissa Spilman
Indexing: Heidi Blough
Production management: Tina Dahl

10 9 8 7 6 5 4 3 2 1
First Edition

This book is affectionately dedicated to my loving wife, Monica, for her patience with my ever-dreaming mind and her unwavering faith, love, and support of those dreams that made this book a reality.

And to the loving memory of Meghan Joyce and to the courage, hope, and inspiration she unselfishly gave to all of us.

1997–2005

CONTENTS

- 11   WELCOME
- 18   SMOKE AND FIRE
- 22   SAUCES AND RUBS
- 26   STARTERS
- 52   SOUPS, SIDES, AND SALADS
- 74   BREADS AND BREAKFAST
- 94   SANDWICHES
- 114   BEEF
- 150   PORK AND LAMB
- 174   POULTRY AND FISH
- 190   THANKSGIVING
- 198   DESSERTS
- 218   ACKNOWLEDGMENTS
- 220   INDEX

UNLIKE MANY COOKBOOK AUTHORS, I am not a classically trained chef or a graduate of culinary school. Everything I know about cooking I learned from family, cookbooks, the Food Network, and good old-fashioned trial and error.

In the interest of full disclosure, I should tell you that in high school I took Home Economics and flunked it—all because of green peas. The teacher told me I had to eat them or fail. Not a hard choice; I despise peas. Instead, I lined them on the rim of my plate and honed my flicking skills by launching them at classmates. You will not find green peas in this cookbook, in any of my restaurants, or in my home, for that matter.

My fascination with food has evolved from flicking peas to an obsessive search for inspiration to create new recipes. I'm constantly seeking unique regional cooking styles in hopes of learning new ways to combine flavors and discovering new ways to use simple, fresh ingredients. Cooking for others brings me immense joy. I'm grateful that life's journey has brought me to a point where I'm fortunate to feed friends every day. So if you've eaten my food *and* bought this book, I am doubly grateful.

SO, WHAT EXACTLY IS A SOUTHERN COWBOY, and what does that have to do with cooking?

If there is one thing that ties the South together more than college football, it's food. Since the Colonial era, the food on the table was a direct reflection of what grew in the fields or grazed in the pastures. Cooks drew from European and African influences, and southern cuisine has since embraced this rich diversity of flavors and styles. This synthesis has blessed us with notable regional specialties—Low Country, Soul, Creole, and a multitude of variations on barbecue. Add in the inspiration brought by an ongoing influx of ethnicities—Spanish, Mexican, Cuban, West Indian—and you have a cuisine that continues to evolve and delight.

Where do barbecue and the art of smoking fit into Southern fare? There's indication that Spanish explorers first encountered what they called *barbacoa* in the Caribbean, likely on the island of Hispaniola, where original inhabitants slow-cooked meats over wooden platforms. By the 1800s, the technique had been popularized throughout the American South, laying the foundation for our most popular culinary legacy.

My own heritage is straight out of the Southern melting pot. One part of my family has roots in the Minorcan Spanish community that established itself in St. Augustine during the late 1700s. Another part hails from the Charleston and Beaufort areas of South Carolina. And yet another came from Lebanon before emigrating to Jacksonville, where I was raised. I grew up in a family who not only knew how to put on a fine spread, but for whom food, family, and hospitality were a way of life. If friends were to drop by unannounced, all activities would stop and an extended greeting would evolve around the breaking of bread.

The same hospitable nature applies to cowboy culture. While I've never herded cattle or spent lonely weeks on the range, I've always been drawn to the cowboy lifestyle. Especially the part that involves sitting around a fire, storytelling, and cooking with friends. While cowboys are most commonly linked in popular imagination with Texas and the West, a number of southern states rank among the top cattle producers. This is especially true of Florida, where 19th-century cattlemen drove herds the length of the state, letting them graze on vast interior grasslands before shipping them out from ports on the Gulf of Mexico. This grueling job often meant tracking down wayward cattle in treacherous swamps and wrangling them back to the herd. That's why in Florida our cowboys were called "cow hunters."

I AM A "BARBECUE HUNTER."

My business career started in Texas, where I met the two great loves of my life—my wife, Monica, and brisket. In that order. Growing up in Jacksonville, my understanding of barbecue was pork and chicken. I had never eaten, let alone heard of, beef brisket until Thanksgiving 1990. Monica took me to Sugarland, Texas, to meet her Uncle Ronnie and Aunt Baby (appropriately named, as she's the youngest of the siblings). It was there that I was introduced to my first succulent slice of heavenly brisket—and her family, of course. It was an epiphany, a revelation. Much to the dismay and ridicule of Monica's cousins, I had never tried anything quite so delicious.

Sensing the essence of my manhood slipping in the eyes of her cousins (who didn't feel the need to hold back), I proceeded to declare that I would learn to smoke the best brisket in North America. Little did I know how difficult brisket is to smoke, let alone how to use a smoker. Blame it on the heightened testosterone levels of a 20-year-old.

After that episode, I threw myself headfirst into smoking in effort to perfect my brisket-cooking technique. It wasn't long before I had a collection of store-bought and home-built smokers welded together with pipes and pulleys that took on the semblance of abstract art (granted, Monica didn't see it quite that way). Working through the meats I quickly learned two things: First, cooking pork is easy. With all the fat, pork is very forgiving. You can make a few mistakes and no one's the wiser. But brisket? That's a whole 'nother animal, excuse the pun. More closely resembling thick leather armor, brisket is a dense slab of meat designed to protect the cow's vitals. Perfecting brisket cooking is a lot like perfecting your golf game—it takes a great deal of patience and finesse. Neither of which I'm good at.

Before retiring as president of a billion-dollar company, I spent 20 years in the healthcare industry. During that time I traveled a lot, which gave me unlimited opportunity to explore barbecue joints throughout the country in my pilgrimage for the best brisket.

To say I pursued it with enthusiasm would be a great understatement. It was not unusual for me to go to a business meeting in say, Memphis and hit three barbecue restaurants before flying home. From Alabama and Tennessee to Georgia and the Carolinas, with occasional forays into such barbecue meccas as Texas and Kansas City, I ate the best 'cue I could find and tried to duplicate my favorites at home. I pursued

Clockwise, from top: John with friend and colleague Jeff Palermo; all four members of the Rivers family at home; table setting at the James Beard House; chatting with guests at the Smokehouse.

LEFT PHOTO BY MELISSA SPILMAN

the perfect brisket with the same tenacity as I did corporate success. I tested the "model" over and over, logging everything in detail from cooking times and temperature variants to weights of meats and rubs. It took me 18 years until I could finally celebrate brisket success. Appropriately, I immediately flew back to Sugarland to put my brisket flag in the ground and put to rest my oath from nearly 20 years earlier.

THE BIRTH OF 4RIVERS SMOKEHOUSE all began with a mistaken phone call and a young girl named Meghan Joyce.

In 2004, a woman called to offer her condolences, having heard that my five-year-old daughter, Cameron, had been diagnosed with cancer. I told her it was a misunderstanding, then quickly hung up and called Monica to confirm that it was indeed a case of mistaken identity. However, I was so shaken by the call and the thought of someone's little girl facing this terrible disease that I set out to find the family and help them any way I could.

Monica and I eventually found Meghan Joyce and her family—parents John and Josie and their two other beautiful daughters, Katie and Sarah. The odd thing about it was that we had no connection whatsoever with their family. Meghan didn't know Cameron, wasn't in her class, and didn't even go to the same school. We didn't work in the same industry, have friends in the same circles, or even live in the same city. There was nothing that would explain why the call came to me in the first place. And to make it even more mysterious, to this day we don't know who the caller was. You see, in my shaken state of mind, I neglected to ask the caller's name. And despite how many times this story has been told over the years, we've never heard from nor identified the caller.

My definition of helping meant doing what felt most natural when comfort was in order—feed those in need. I offered to help organize a barbecue at Meghan's church to raise money for her treatment. Now, up to that point, I had only cooked for backyard parties of 20 or so folks, and it didn't always turn out so

From left: The original 4 Rivers Smokehouse location, circa 2009, before and after.

well. When 450 RSVPs came in, I wasn't so sure I could pull it off, especially since I had only 10 days to prepare. An amazing team of families came together and made it a wonderful evening for Meghan and her family. I like to say that it was by the grace of God that the fundraiser was a success, the food was well received, and, much to my relief, no one got sick.

That single event ignited a passion. I already loved to cook, but thought, can I do what I love and help people at the same time? Thus began what we dubbed our Barbecue Ministry.

Along with friends, family, and a growing team of volunteers, for the next four years I cooked for pretty much anyone who asked and needed help—schools, churches, charities, civic organizations, people in distress. I was still working fulltime, but evenings and weekends were devoted to the ministry. Our garage kept filling up with more and more equipment, and at one point Monica jokingly suggested that the only reason I was doing this was because it gave me an excuse for buying bigger smokers (she's a pretty smart one).

We branched out with a chili-cookoff team and also began donating bottles of my "For Goodness Sake BBQ Sauce" to our children's school, which sold them for $5 apiece in the after-school pick-up line. Practice and fine-tuning not only increased my smoking skills but further spread the word of the Barbecue Ministry. In 2008, we estimate that we fed almost 70,000 people ... out of our garage.

Quite obviously, we needed more space, which is what led us to a former "Just Brakes" shop on Fairbanks Avenue in Winter Park, Florida. The original idea was that it would be a commissary for our charitable work, but during the renovation I came up with the idea of building a serving counter on the off chance that people might want to buy leftovers from the weekend's charity events or even order takeout.

Little did I imagine …

WE OPENED OUR FIRST 4RIVERS SMOKEHOUSE in that tiny 1,100-square-foot space in Winter Park on October 26, 2009 with 12 employees, which included Monica and myself. The morning was surprisingly hot for October. I recall this vividly because the AC broke, as did most of the used equipment we'd scraped together. We were out of money so we couldn't advertise. There was no grand opening, no promotions, no giant blow-up animals, no people waving signs. Just good old-fashioned word of mouth and a whole lot of prayer. We had no idea what to expect. I just hoped somebody would stop by.

Uncermoniously and with great trepidation, we unlocked the door and turned on the "Hot Brisket Now" sign at 11 a.m. By 11:30 we had a line out the door. By noon, the line extended into the parking lot. Within the month, word had spread so much that the daily line snaked around the building. Now, less than four years later, we have five locations and more than 500 amazing folks on our 4 Rivers team.

To this day, the Barbecue Ministry remains our foundation and focus. And to this day, we have never advertised, never had a grand opening, and never made much of a commotion other than telling folks we were opening and then simply unlocking the door at 11 a.m. and turning on the "Hot Brisket Now" sign. To say that our prayers were heard would be an understatement.

FROM THE BEGINNING, my mantra has been to de-regionalize and break down the boundaries of barbecue. I believe if you provide down-home, not-fancy-yet-high-quality good food, people will come. When I first shared that I was making Texas-style brisket our specialty and lead item, people scoffed and told me I would fail. No one had ever succeeded serving brisket in the pork-loving Deep South. So far, we've proved the naysayers wrong. Brisket represents the majority of our sales, with each store smoking 10,000-plus pounds a week, contributing to the over 1 million pounds we'll smoke in 2013.

Beyond the Texas-influenced brisket, my recipes take inspiration from my many years of traveling during my healthcare career. My pulled pork comes from Alabama, ribs from the Carolinas, burnt-ends from Kansas City, chicken from Georgia, and tri-tip from California.

While *The Southern Cowboy Cookbook* includes many of the favorite dishes from the Smokehouse menu, it also expands upon the concept of down-home comfort food. In these pages you'll find my homage to everything from cheese grits and gumbo to skillet cornbread and pecan pie.

So, please gather around the fire, cowboys, and enjoy yourselves. I sure do appreciate you taking a look at my first cookbook.

BLESSINGS,

John Rivers

Clockwise from top: Lining up, inside and outside the Winter Park Smokehouse; our famous sign says it all.

TOP PHOTOS BY JON WHITTLE

SMOKE & FIRE

THERE ARE AS MANY TALES about the origins of barbecue as there are types of sauces. The prevailing account is that Christopher Columbus first discovered native inhabitants cooking meats over indirect flames on a Caribbean island he named Hispaniola (present-day Haiti and the Dominican Republic). The allure of preparing and preserving meats with smoke, called *barbacoa*, fascinated the Spaniards and grew in use and legend as the conquistador expeditions proceeded across North America. And it was adapted by Native Americans, who smoked fish hung from the tops of teepees, likely as way to keep flies away during the drying and cooking process.

You can still find old BBQ joints where meats are smoked over glowing embers from dried hardwood that has been stacked high and allowed to burn down before being shoveled into a pit under the meat. The lingering smoke from the embers imparts the distinctive scent recognized as the hallmark of an accomplished pitmaster. While there are various way to impart smoke flavor on a gas grill, including chips, pellets, and liquid smoke, nothing can duplicate the true essence of wood and explains my personal prejudice for wood fires over gas.

Fuel sources such as wood, charcoal, and propane each produce different flavors

that result from their makeup of combustible by-products. Within them there are dozens of microscopic compounds that include solids (char, creosote, ash), gases (carbon monoxide, carbon dioxide, nitrogen oxide), and liquids (water vapor, phenols).

The unique combination of compounds of each particular fuel source is influenced greatly by the speed at which it is released or, in other words, its heat and temperature. A piece of soaked hickory heated at a low temperature for an extended period is going to produce different flavors than charcoal or propane burning at a higher temperature. Smoke is simply the vehicle that carries the flavor compounds to the meat. The amino acids in the proteins of the meat allow the compounds to stick as the smoke envelops the meat.

How much of each flavor compound resides in the smoke depends on the:
- Composition (type of wood, charcoal, pellets)
- Rate of combustion (heat or temperature)
- Amount of oxygen available (the venting)

Probably 90 percent of the best steakhouses grill with gas for a single reason: Gas broilers can reach the higher temperature needed to create a sear hot enough to char the outside of a steak without overcooking the inside. The char forms a crust that acts as a barrier protecting the juices in the center of the steak.

While propane releases combustible compounds, they are far less complex than wood or charcoal compounds and, as result, significantly lower in flavor. Even if you put wood chips on an electric coil or in a smoke box in your grill, the flavor is vastly different because propane still remains the primary source of heat—and thus, is generating mostly flavorless compounds. The wood chips themselves contribute very little heat comparatively, so they have a lesser impact on flavor.

At the end of the day, the most distinct flavor is produced when wood is used as the primary source of heat. Just as with sauces and rubs, regional influences determine the type of wood used for smoking. For Texas barbecue, mesquite is far and away the favorite, but it can be overpowering if not used with restraint. Oak is a good choice for thick cuts that require longer cooking times, since it burns slowly and imparts a mild flavor. My preference is hickory. Its sweet flavor nicely complements everything from beef and pork to poultry, offering a distinct result that doesn't overpower the meat.

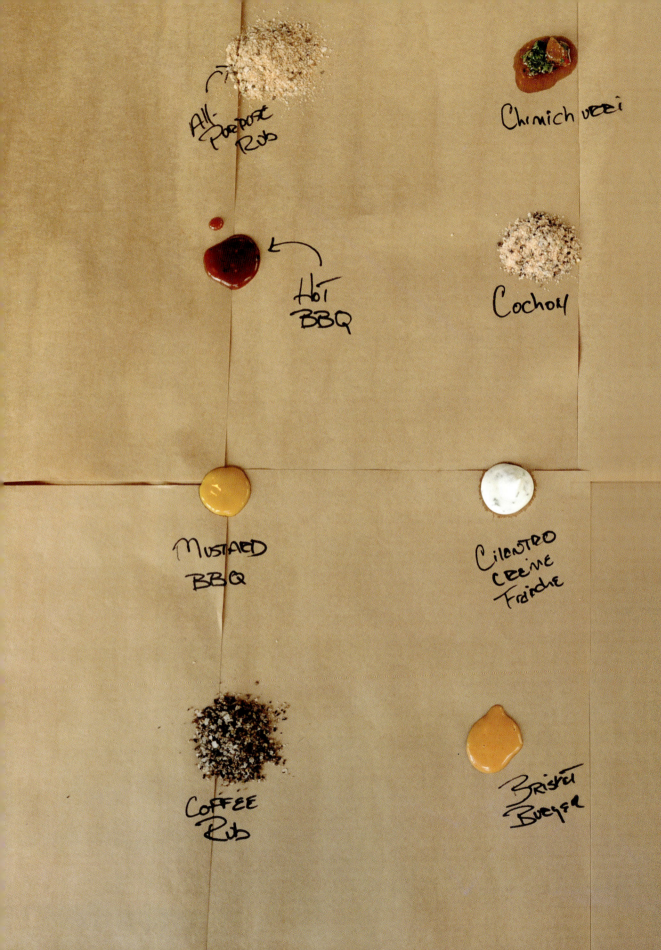

SAUCES & RUBS

ONE OF MY GOALS at the Smokehouse is to introduce BBQ flavors and styles from multiple regions to my guests. I recognize that regional prejudices exist, but I believe that people appreciate well-prepared, high-quality BBQ regardless of where they live.

That said, it's important to recognize the regional variations in both the meats smoked and the sauces and rubs used throughout the "BBQ Belt." As BBQ spread from the Caribbean through North America, settlers adapted it as their primary means of preserving meats and fish. With the westward expansion, smoking was introduced to the different European communities that had settled throughout the South. Each influenced the flavors of the sauces and rubs to more closely align with those of their homeland tastes. And thus, regional BBQ was born.

The vinegar sauce of North Carolina traces back to British colonists and their fondness for tart flavors. The mustard sauce of South Carolina originated with communities of French and German immigrants and their penchant for mustard. The thick molasses and tomato-based style of Memphis BBQ stemmed from the city's status as a Mississippi River port and the abundance of molasses that passed through on ships. German families in the Carolinas eventually moved west into Texas to cultivate cattle, bringing with them the Caribbean/Spanish/Carolina technique of smoking meats. The scarcity of hogs led to the introduction of BBQ beef and the rise of smoked brisket. They were joined by large numbers of Czech immigrants who introduced yet another BBQ staple to the region—smoked sausage. A thinner, less sweet yet hardy tomato-based sauce evolved as a result of the abundance of tomato farms throughout Texas. As for Kansas City's sweet-tart sauce, it likely arose when BBQ pioneer Henry Perry moved there in the early 1900s and created a sauce that brought together the tartness of the Carolinas, the sweetness of Memphis, and the tomato and beef flavors of Texas.

In any event, we celebrate all regional flavors at the Smokehouse and here are three go-to recipes that are called on throughout this book, along with Mustard BBQ Sauce, a favorite among many of our guests.

MUSTARD BBQ SAUCE

MAKES ABOUT 2½ CUPS

1 cup yellow mustard

1 tablespoon ketchup

½ cup brown sugar, tightly packed

¼ cup cider vinegar

1 tablespoon Worcestershire sauce

¼ cup water

1 tablespoon coarsely ground black pepper

1 tablespoon kosher salt

4 tablespoons (½ stick) salted butter, melted

½ teaspoon cayenne pepper

½ teaspoon granulated garlic

1 tablespoon lemon juice

Whisk together all ingredients in a bowl until well incorporated.

Can be stored in refrigerator for 1 week.

ALL-PURPOSE RUB

MAKES ABOUT ½ CUP

2 tablespoons freshly ground black pepper

3 tablespoons coarse salt

3 tablespoons brown sugar

1½ teaspoons garlic powder

½ teaspoon chili powder

½ teaspoon onion powder

1 teaspoon dry mustard

½ teaspoon ground red pepper

Mix ingredients in a small bowl. Store in airtight container.

BRISKET RUB

MAKES ¼ CUP

2 tablespoons freshly ground black pepper

1 teaspoon garlic powder

1 teaspoon dried parsley

1 teaspoon oregano

1 teaspoon coarse salt

1 teaspoon onion powder

1 teaspoon chili powder

1 teaspoon sugar

Mix ingredients in a small bowl. Store in airtight container.

ALL-PURPOSE BBQ SAUCE

MAKES ABOUT 2½ CUPS

1 cup ketchup

⅓ cup yellow mustard (like French's)

½ cup brown sugar, tightly packed

2 tablespoons cider vinegar

2 tablespoons Worcestershire sauce

2 tablespoons water

½ tablespoon kosher salt

½ tablespoon coarsely ground black pepper

4 tablespoons (½ stick) salted butter

1 large garlic clove, minced

⅓ cup Vidalia onion, grated

¼ tablespoon cayenne pepper

¼ tablespoon chili powder

Whisk ketchup, mustard, brown sugar, vinegar, Worcestershire, water, salt, and pepper together in a bowl.

Heat butter in a medium saucepan over medium heat until shimmering. Add onion and garlic and sauté until onion is translucent, 3 to 4 minutes.

Stir in chili powder and cayenne and cook until fragrant, about 1 minute.

Whisk in ketchup mix and bring to a boil. Reduce heat to medium-low and simmer gently for 30 minutes until sauce turns a darker shade of brown.

Can be stored in refrigerator for 1 week. For best results, warm over low heat before serving.

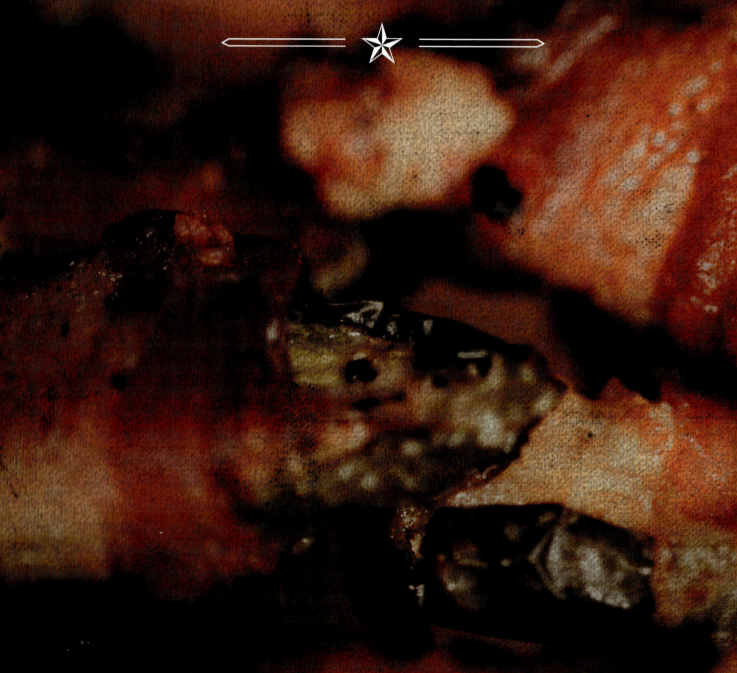
STARTERS

SMOKED CHICKEN WINGS

ON ONE OF THE first dates with my future wife, Monica, we ordered chicken wings. I knew right then that I would marry her. She only ate the drumettes, while I preferred the wingettes. I figured that was all I needed to know to make a lifelong commitment.

The biggest difference between these wings and traditional fried wings is that the smoke and the rub drive the flavor, rather than depending on the sauce for flavor. In addition, smoking produces plumper and moister wings, and is better for you. I consider this our healthy alternative at the Smokehouse. **MAKES 2 DOZEN WINGS**

INGREDIENTS

¼ cup sugar

½ cup chili powder

½ cup All-Purpose Rub (page 25)

24 whole chicken wings, cut into drumette and wingette pieces

1 cup All-Purpose BBQ Sauce (page 25)

½ cup ranch or blue cheese dressing, for dipping

METHOD

Light a smoker using hickory wood and allow temperature to settle at 305°F.

Combine sugar, chili powder, and All-Purpose Rub in a large bowl. Sprinkle over wings to thoroughly coat.

Smoke at 305°F for 45 minutes.

Just before serving, light a gas grill and heat to medium high.

Toss wings in BBQ sauce and "flash" on grill to allow sauce to caramelize, 3 minutes on each side. Flip only once.

Serve hot with ranch or blue cheese dipping sauce.

SIX SHOOTER

THE SIX SHOOTER was a result of my attempt to create an alternative to the spill-prone pulled pork sandwich at "fussy" catering events. The endeavor truly brought appreciation to the term "putting perfume on a pig."

True to its name, the final creation consists of six ingredients that present beautifully in a shot or parfait glass while providing layers of offsetting, yet complementing flavors. It quickly grew in popularity and successfully elevates the otherwise humble pulled pork to an elegant level. I suspect we'll see this served at the French Laundry any day now. **MAKES 1 SERVING**

INGREDIENTS

⅓ cup Baked Cheese Grits (page 70)

½ cup Pulled Pork (page 152)

⅓ cup Southern coleslaw (page 57)

2 to 3 pickled jalapeño slices

2 to 3 dill pickle slices

2 tablespoons All-Purpose BBQ Sauce (page 25)

METHOD

In a parfait glass, layer in order the cheese grits, a thin layer of BBQ sauce, pulled pork, and coleslaw. Top with jalapeños and pickles, and drizzle with more sauce.

CARNE ASADA NACHOS

I LIKE NACHOS piled high and messy, but Monica prefers hers simple and neat. This was an attempt at a compromise. The result is a neatly stacked nacho piled high with a lot of flavor. You can use any kind of steak or beef cut, but we like beef short ribs to add a richer beef flavor to the dish. **MAKES 20**

NACHOS

4 Smoked Beef Short Ribs (page 148), or grilled steak

1¼ cups refried beans, canned

20 (2-inch) round tortilla chips

1¼ cups Mexican-blend shredded cheese

20 slices pickled jalapeños

PICO DE GALLO

5 whole plum tomatoes, diced

1 medium sweet onion, diced

2 whole jalapeños, seeds removed and diced

1 bunch cilantro, destemmed and roughly chopped

1 lime, halved

Salt to taste

CILANTRO LIME CREME FRAICHE

1 cup heavy cream

2 tablespoons buttermilk

2 tablespoons plain yogurt

¼ cup chopped cilantro

Juice and zest of ½ lime

MAKE CREME FRAICHE

Combine cream, buttermilk, and yogurt in mixing bowl. Beat or hand whisk until soft peaks form. Stir in cilantro and lime. Cover and refrigerate until ready to use.

MAKE PICO DE GALLO

Combine first 4 ingredients in a small bowl. Squeeze juice from lime into the mixture. Add salt to taste and mix well.

MAKE NACHOS

Cut meat into 2-by-2-inch pieces. Preheat broiler. Spread 1 tablespoon refried beans on each chip. Top with piece of rib meat and sprinkle with cheese. Broil for 2 minutes or until cheese is melted. Remove from oven and top each chip with pico de gallo, crème fraîche, and a slice of jalapeño.

GRILLED BRISKET, ASIAGO, AND JALAPEÑO PIZZA

MY FIRST JOB was washing dishes at a pizza place called The Loop in the San Marco neighborhood of Jacksonville, near where I grew up. Along with teaching me the value of hard work, the owner, Mike Schneider, introduced me to Chicago-style pizza and another personal favorite, the Chicago Dog.

The idea of grilling pizza may be intimidating, but it's actually pretty easy and a lot of fun to do with the family. Subbing BBQ sauce for tomato sauce was the start of my contribution to this Italian/Chicago classic. Topping it with smoked brisket made it a Smokehouse classic, too. **MAKES 1 PIZZA**

INGREDIENTS

1 large Vidalia onion

3 tablespoons vegetable oil, for grilling and sautéing, divided

½ cup flour

Prepared pizza dough (typically found in the bakery section of the supermarket)

Nonstick cooking spray

All-Purpose BBQ Sauce (page 25)

½ cup mozzarella cheese

½ cup shredded Mexican cheese mix, or pepper jack cheese

¼ pound thinly sliced Brisket, slightly warmed (page 116)

1 fresh tomato, thinly sliced

1 whole jalapeño, or 2 tablespoons pickled

½ cup shredded Asiago

Freshly grated Parmesan

METHOD

Thinly slice and sauté onion with 1 tablespoon oil in saucepan over low heat until caramelized, about 30 minutes.

Light a grill, close lid, and allow to heat to medium-high.

Rub a rolling pin with flour. Sprinkle flour on a flat working surface and roll pizza dough to desired thickness to form a circle.

Spray grill with nonstick spray.

Lightly brush one side of pizza dough with vegetable oil and place on grill, oil side down. Grill 3 to 5 minutes with lid open until bottom of dough is browned and crispy.

Using a large spatula, remove crust from grill and slide onto a baking sheet.

TIP

When caramelizing the onion, which gives this pizza its sweet finish, you can't rush things. Be patient and allow the onion to cook low and slow until it reaches a deep golden brown.

Lightly brush uncooked side with oil and flip over so grilled side is now facing up.

On grilled side, layer ingredients in the following order: BBQ sauce, mozzarella cheese, Mexican/pepper jack cheese, brisket, onion, tomato, jalapeño, Asiago.

Using the baking sheet, transfer pizza to hot grill by carefully sliding the pie off the baking sheet, starting with the side farthest away from you while pulling the pan toward you.

Close lid and grill for 5 to 7 minutes on low until bottom is crisp and cheese is melted. If bottom is cooking too fast, slide pie to the unlit side of the grill, using spatula.

Remove from grill and cool 1 to 2 minutes before cutting.

Top with Parmesan just before serving.

DIABLO SHRIMP WITH FRIED GREEN TOMATOES AND MANGO SALSA

NO SOUTHERN COOKBOOK worth its salt is complete without at least one fried green tomato dish. This recipe pairs the tartness of the green tomato with the fire of the cayenne shrimp, which is offset by the coolness of the mango salsa. When you bite into it you experience all four seasons of taste sensations—hot, tart, cool, and crunch. **MAKES 16 APPETIZERS**

MANGO SALSA

1 large mango, diced

1 tomato, diced

¼ red onion, diced

½ cup cilantro, chopped

¼ cup diced red bell pepper

¼ cup diced cucumber

2 tablespoons jalapeños, chopped

2 tablespoons fresh lime juice

4 teaspoons olive oil

Coarse salt and freshly ground black pepper, to taste

FRIED GREEN TOMATOES

1½ cups plus 2 teaspoons sugar

1½ cups water

3 green tomatoes

¼ cup plus 1 tablespoon cilantro, chopped

2 cups coarse cornmeal

2 teaspoons freshly ground black pepper

2 teaspoons coarse salt

½ teaspoon cayenne pepper

½ teaspoon granulated garlic

2 large eggs

2 cups buttermilk

1 teaspoon hot sauce

Vegetable oil, for frying

DIABLO SHRIMP

16 jumbo shrimp, peeled and deveined

6 tablespoons fish sauce

4 tablespoons vegetable oil

2 teaspoons turmeric

2 jalapeño peppers, seeds removed, chopped

3 red chili peppers, seeds removed, chopped

2 Anaheim peppers, seeds removed, chopped

1 tomatillo, cleaned and quartered

8 small cloves garlic, finely chopped

1 cup chopped onion

⅓ cup chopped cilantro

2 (1-inch) pieces ginger, peeled

2 tablespoons light brown sugar

1 tablespoon chili sauce

½ tablespoon fresh lime juice

CONTINUED

MAKE SALSA

Combine all ingredients in a bowl; refrigerate 1 hour or until ready to serve.

MAKE FRIED GREEN TOMATOES

Combine 1½ cups sugar with water and bring to a boil. Reduce heat and simmer until sugar dissolves, 1 to 2 minutes. Remove from heat and refrigerate to cool completely. Can be done ahead.

Cut tomatoes into 16 (¼-inch) slices. Combine cooled sugar water and cilantro in a large bowl; add sliced tomatoes and marinate for 30 minutes at room temperature.

Mix together cornmeal, pepper, salt, cayenne, garlic, and remaining sugar in a shallow bowl.

Whisk together eggs, buttermilk, and hot sauce in a mixing bowl.

Cover bottom of a heavy skillet with ½ inch of oil, then place over medium-high heat.

Lightly coat tomato slices with cornmeal mixture, then egg mixture, then back to cornmeal mixture.

Fry tomatoes on each side until golden brown, about 2 to 3 minutes. Drain on paper towels and keep warm.

MAKE SHRIMP

Place all ingredients other than shrimp in a food processor or blender and coarsely chop.

Divide sauce into equal parts and set half aside for later use. Add shrimp to the other half, toss to coat, and marinate for 30 minutes, refrigerated.

Remove shrimp and discard marinade. Grill shrimp for 1 to 2 minutes on each side, being careful not to overcook.

ASSEMBLE

Place a tablespoon of mango salsa on each fried tomato. Top with 1 or 2 shrimp and 1 tablespoon of the reserved sauce.

John and Jeff on opening day of the Winter Park Smokehouse, October 26, 2009

HICKORY-SMOKED, RIOJA-INFUSED MANCHEGO CROQUETTES

I'M A BIG FAN OF Spanish-style tapas, which might be attributed to the Spanish side of my heritage or simply to the fact that tapas are just so good. This recipe began with the simple question: What would happen if we soaked cheese in wine, then smoked it? After plenty of trial and error, we wound up with a richly flavored cheese croquette that we topped with a sweet and salty vinaigrette laced with honey and olives to balance the flavors. **MAKES 24 CROQUETTES**

SMOKED MANCHEGO

1½ pounds manchego cheese

1½ cups Rioja wine

¾ cup flour

1 egg

½ cup water

¾ cup panko bread crumbs

¾ cup ground almonds

Olive oil, for frying

Coarse salt

SMOKED OLIVES

24 queen olives, pitted

Juice and zest of 1 lemon

¼ cup garlic, minced

1 small jalapeño, seeded and minced

¼ cup parsley, chopped

¼ cup cilantro, chopped

1 cup olive oil

ROASTED GARLIC HONEY VINAIGRETTE

3 to 4 cloves garlic, roasted and peeled

¼ cup red wine vinegar

2 tablespoons balsamic vinegar

2 teaspoons sherry vinegar

2 tablespoons honey

½ cup extra virgin olive oil

2 teaspoons sugar

1½ teaspoons spicy brown mustard

½ cup tomatoes, chopped

2 tablespoons fresh basil, thinly sliced

¼ teaspoon salt

½ teaspoon coarsely ground black pepper

MAKE SMOKED MANCHEGO

Remove skin from cheese and cut into 1½-inch cubes. Place in a zip-top bag with wine and marinate, refrigerated, for at least 3 hours or overnight.

Spread foil over a portion of a smoker's rack, to fit the cheese.

Preheat smoker to 200°F using charcoal and soaked hickory wood.

Remove cheese from marinade and place in smoker. Begin to check cheese after 15 minutes; remove from smoker at 30 minutes, or when cheese is soft and lightly browned. Wrap cheese in plastic wrap, twisting ends to form a log. Refrigerate for at least 30 minutes to harden.

Meanwhile, measure flour into a small bowl. In a second bowl, whisk together egg and water to make an egg wash. Combine panko and almonds in a third dish.

Coat each piece of cheese by first gently pressing in flour. Dip in egg wash, then panko-almond mixture, gently pressing so that crumbs stick. Wrap in plastic wrap and refrigerate until ready to fry. Can be made up to 3 days in advance.

When ready to serve, heat ¼ inch of olive oil over moderately high heat in a large skillet until shimmering. Add cheese to hot oil and fry until golden and crisp, about 2 to 3 minutes. Drain on a rack and season lightly with salt.

MAKE SMOKED OLIVES

Preheat smoker to 200°F, using charcoal and soaked hickory wood.

Drain olives and wrap in cheesecloth. Place olives in smoker and smoke them for 30 minutes.

Meanwhile, combine lemon juice and zest, garlic, jalapeño, parsley, cilantro, and 1 cup olive oil in a large bowl.

Remove olives from smoker and discard cheesecloth. Add to mixture, cover, refrigerate, and allow to marinate for up to 24 hours.

Before serving, rinse olives and mix with olive oil. If not using immediately, cover and refrigerate until ready to serve.

MAKE VINAIGRETTE

Place all ingredients in a blender and blend until smooth.

ASSEMBLE

Spear a smoked olive with a toothpick and place on top of a warm manchego croquette. Drizzle with vinaigrette.

BACON-WRAPPED SMOKED JALAPEÑOS

THIS IS OUR TWIST on the popular jalapeño poppers, or armadillo eggs, as they're referred to in Texas. I found smoking the jalapeño mellowed the heat and produced a more distinct, sweet flavor that blended well with the smoky saltiness of the bacon. Every once in a while one flares up and reminds you that it's a jalapeño, but for the most part, it's an appetizer even non-fire eaters can enjoy. **MAKES 20**

INGREDIENTS

10 medium jalapeño peppers

½ cup whipped cream cheese, allowed to reach room temperature

10 slices hickory-smoked bacon, halved

METHOD

Chop tops and stems off peppers, slice lengthwise, and scrape out seeds and white membrane using a teaspoon (a grapefruit spoon works best). You may want to wear latex gloves to protect your fingers from the heat.

Using a small spoon or butter knife, fill the cavity of each pepper with whipped cream cheese. Be careful not to overstuff.

Wrap each with ½ slice of bacon, starting and ending at underside of pepper so the two ends of the bacon overlap and the weight of the stuffed pepper sits atop the seam holding it together.

Smoke on a grill at 225°F for about 45 minutes to an hour or until bacon is cooked.

TIP

You'll lose the smoky flavor, but in a pinch you can make these in the oven. Place the wrapped jalapeños on a broiler pan or a cookie cooling rack in a baking pan, so the peppers don't sit in the bacon grease, and bake at 250°F for 30 minutes or until the bacon is done. Don't be tempted to increase the temperature, as it will only cause the cheese to melt and run out.

BBQ QUESADILLA

A FEW CHRISTMASES AGO. I went through a quesadilla obsession. Much to my wife's dismay, I purchased six quesadilla makers that I deemed necessary for "R & D." The beauty of the quesadilla is its versatility of combinations and the fun involved in experimenting with different flavors. Though I don't necessarily want to recall all of the combinations we made in our "research," I do recall with great fondness all the fun times grilling quesadillas with my children and their friends.

After extensive trial and error with BBQ flavors, simplicity once again proved best. I hope you enjoy our BBQ Quesadillas as much as my family does. **MAKES 1**

INGREDIENTS

1 (10-inch) flour tortilla

5 ounces warm beef brisket, smoked chicken, or pork

4 tablespoons All-Purpose BBQ Sauce (page 25)

½ cup shredded cheddar cheese

Vegetable oil, for grilling

Sour cream (for garnish)

Sliced jalapeños (for garnish)

METHOD

Heat grill (or stovetop grill) to medium-high. Lay tortilla on a flat working surface.

Spread brisket, chicken, or pork on half of the tortilla, leaving ½ inch of uncovered space on the outside rim. Press meat down so it adheres tightly on tortilla. This will prevent it from falling out while grilling.

Drizzle with BBQ sauce and top with cheese.

Fold tortilla in half so the cheese side remains on top, and press outer rim down to create a seam. Lightly brush top half of tortilla with oil and place on hot grill, oiled (cheese) side down.

Grill 2 minutes, rotate 90 degrees, and grill for another 2 minutes. Flip and repeat until cheese melts.

Allow to cool for a couple of minutes before cutting into wedges.

To get the full quesadilla experience, top with a dollop of sour cream, a slice of jalapeño, and a touch of BBQ sauce.

BRISKET BRUSCHETTA

WHEN FRIENDS INVITED US to cater a political event, they asked me to create a menu of what they described as "fancy BBQ." It was a fun challenge transforming our traditional BBQ specialties into more elegant finger foods while maintaining the integrity of the Smokehouse. Once the wheels started turning, we came up with all kinds of interesting combinations—brisket carpaccio, smoked prime rib–wrapped asparagus, and brisket empanadas ... to name just a few. However, the hit of the party was the Brisket Bruschetta. The sweet and peppery flavors of the smoked tomato jam combined with the rich, smoky flavor of brisket resulted in unique layers of flavor that brought brisket to a whole new level. Added benefit: You can eat it with one hand. **MAKES ABOUT 24 PIECES**

SMOKED TOMATO JAM
Makes 1¾ cups

2¼ pounds tomatoes (about 6 medium)

1½ cups sugar

3 tablespoons fresh lime juice

1½ tablespoons fresh ginger, grated

1½ tablespoons garlic, minced

1 teaspoon ground cumin

¼ teaspoon ground cinnamon

Pinch of ground cloves

2 jalapeños, seeds and white membrane removed, finely chopped

BRISKET BRUSCHETTA

1 loaf crusty French bread

¼ cup extra-virgin olive oil

1½ pounds warm smoked brisket, sliced medium thick

24 basil leaves

MAKE SMOKED TOMATO JAM

Wash tomatoes, place in a pan, and put in smoker at 225°F for 30 to 40 minutes, or until skins start to break. Remove from smoker and cool.

Remove and discard skins and seeds from smoked tomatoes; coarsely chop the tomato pulp.

Combine tomatoes and remaining ingredients in a heavy saucepan over medium heat. Bring to a boil, stirring often. Reduce heat and simmer, stirring occasionally, until mixture is the consistency of thick jam, about 1 hour and 15 minutes. Color will be deep red. Refrigerate until ready to use.

MAKE BRUSCHETTA

Preheat oven to 325°F.

Slice French bread into ½-inch-thick slices on the diagonal.

Using a pastry brush, coat one side of each slice with olive oil and place on a baking sheet, oiled side up.

Bake about 3 minutes or until golden brown. Remove from oven.

ASSEMBLE

Top bread with warm brisket and add a dollop of jam. Garnish with basil leaf.

TEQUILA-SPIKED QUESO FUNDIDO CON CHORIZO

THOUGH A RELATIVELY simple dish, properly executed queso fundido (Spanish for "melted cheese") is the mark of authenticity in Mexican restaurants and a go-to appetizer for me and my head of operations and good friend, Jeff Palermo. Oaxaca cheese (asadero) and Chihuahua cheese are traditional, but other cheeses that remain stringy when melted, such as whole-milk mozzerella, may be used.

This particular recipe owes a tip of the hat to Food Network's Aarón Sánchez, who approached this classic by incorporating another Mexican favorite—tequila. When this photo was taken of us at the 2013 South Beach Wine and Food Festival, I told Aarón I had used his recipe as an inspiration for my version of fundido. He summed up his approval in one word: "Respect!" **SERVES 6 TO 8**

PHOTO BY MICHAEL PISARRI

INGREDIENTS

1 fresh poblano, stem removed

6 ounces pork or beef chorizo, casings removed

½ cup white onion, sliced into ½-inch strips

½ cup tequila

14 ounces Oaxaca (asadero), Chihuahua, or queso quesadilla cheese, shredded (about 4 cups)

1 small tomato, cored, seeded, and cut into ¼-inch dice

2 tablespoons fresh cilantro, chopped

Warm tortillas and tortilla chips, for serving

METHOD

Grill poblano on all sides until outer skin is blackened. This can be done over an open flame of a gas oven or broiled in the oven. Place charred poblano in a brown paper bag, close bag, and allow to sit unopened for 20 minutes for the skin to separate or "sweat" from the poblano.

Remove poblano from bag. Slice one side vertically from top to bottom, remove seeds, and lay on a flat surface in one whole piece with the charred side up. Using the flat side of a knife, scrape the charred skin off, leaving the bright green flesh of the poblano exposed. Cut into thin 1-inch strips and set aside.

Preheat oven to 350°F. Cook chorizo in a skillet over medium heat until almost crisp; drain on paper towels and set aside.

Wipe out skillet, leaving a scant amount of grease. Sauté onions over medium heat until tender, about 5 minutes, adding poblano for last 2 minutes to reheat.

Remove pan from heat and stir in tequila. Return to heat and simmer, uncovered, until tequila evaporates, about 5 minutes. Remove from heat.

Pour tequila-onion-poblano mixture into a large bowl and stir in cheese and cooked chorizo. Transfer to an 8-by-8-inch baking dish and bake, uncovered, 20 minutes, or until cheese is bubbling and golden.

Remove from oven and sprinkle with tomato and cilantro. Serve with warm tortillas and tortilla chips.

SOUPS, SIDES AND SALADS

SMOKED CHICKEN AND SAUSAGE GUMBO

INFLUENCED BY EMERIL LAGASSE, born out of my deep affinity for Cajun food, and perfected by Jeff's many years of cooking while in New Orleans, this recipe introduces a Smokehouse undertone to the classic Cajun staple. Topping it with fried okra adds a much-appreciated crunch to what can otherwise become a slimy gumbo. It's a nice final touch that helps this gumbo stand apart.

SERVES 10 TO 12

INGREDIENTS

1 (5-pound) smoked pork shoulder, shredded

1 cup rendered juice and scraps from the pork shoulder

1 large Vidalia onion, finely chopped

2 celery hearts, finely chopped

1 large green pepper, finely chopped

¼ cup Cajun seasoning, such as Paul Prudhomme's Magic

2 pounds sausage, such as an andouille or other smoked sausage, thinly sliced

1 cup (2 sticks) butter

1 cup all-purpose flour

8 garlic cloves, roughly chopped

2 cups beef broth

½ teaspoon cayenne pepper

1 (14.5-ounce) can stewed tomatoes

1 (3-pound) Smoked Chicken, skin removed, meat pulled from bones and chopped, skin and bones discarded (page 186)

½ cup chopped scallions

1 teaspoon filé powder

Hot sauce, to taste

FOR ASSEMBLY

4-5 cups cooked white rice

Fresh parsley, chopped

Fried Okra (page 57)

METHOD

If pork shoulder is hot off the smoker, allow to cool before shredding (can be done up to a week in advance). Reserve juices and scraps.

Place onion, celery, and green pepper in a bowl and sprinkle with Cajun seasoning. Blend well and set aside.

Sauté sausage in a large, heavy-bottomed stockpot over medium heat until golden. Remove sausage with a slotted spoon and transfer to a plate lined with paper towels. Leave rendered oil in pot for roux.

Over medium heat, add butter to pot, stirring until melted. Turn heat to low and slowly sprinkle in flour, whisking until mixture is smooth. Cook, stirring constantly, until mixture is chocolate brown, about 15 minutes. Do not rush this step, stop whisking, or walk away from the pan. If you do, the roux will burn before you know it.

Add seasoned vegetables to roux and sauté 5 minutes. Add garlic and sauté for another 5 minutes, adding a splash of broth to moisten vegetables if needed.

Add broth in ½-cup increments, whisking to blend, and simmer for 5 minutes between each addition to allow base to thicken. Continue in stages for remaining broth.

Bring to a boil, then reduce heat to medium-low and simmer, covered, 1 hour.

Stir in cayenne and stewed tomatoes. Simmer, uncovered, 1 hour, stirring occasionally.

Add chicken, shredded pork, and reserved sausage. Stir in scallions, filé, rendered pork juice (with scraps), and hot sauce to taste. Simmer, uncovered, 30 to 45 minutes more, stirring occasionally.

Serve gumbo over cooked white rice, and top with fried okra, chopped parsley, and a dab of hot sauce.

TIP

The key to good gumbo is in the roux, which in simple terms is equal parts butter or oil and flour, well incorporated and cooked slowly to the desired doneness or shade of brown. The color of the roux will change from white (used in a béchamel sauce) to blond to caramel to a dark chocolate brown, which is what we prefer in this recipe. For a darker roux, you'll need to cook it longer and at a lower heat to prevent it from burning.

SOUPS, SIDES, AND SALADS

MAPLE-GLAZED CARROTS

SERVES 6 TO 8

INGREDIENTS

4 tablespoons unsalted butter

2 pounds baby carrots

4 tablespoons maple syrup, divided

½ teaspoon kosher salt, plus additional to taste

4 tablespoons sherry vinegar, divided

4 teaspoons chopped flat-leaf parsley, divided

Freshly ground black pepper, to taste

METHOD

Melt butter in a large sauté pan over medium heat. Add carrots, 2 tablespoons maple syrup, and salt. Sauté until carrots are coated with butter mixture, about 1 minute.

Add 2 tablespoons sherry vinegar and enough water to almost cover carrots; cover and bring to a boil over high heat. Boil, covered, 2 minutes. Uncover and boil until liquid is reduced to syrup and carrots are tender, stirring often, about 10 minutes.

Add remaining 2 tablespoons maple syrup and 2 tablespoons vinegar to carrots and toss over medium-high heat until carrots are thickly coated with glaze, about 3 minutes. Stir in 2 teaspoons parsley. Season carrots to taste with more salt and a generous amount of pepper.

Transfer carrots to a serving bowl and sprinkle with remaining 2 teaspoons parsley.

SOUTHERN COLESLAW

JUST LIKE SALSA in a Mexican restaurant, coleslaw is a telltale sign of a good BBQ joint. I prefer my slaw finely chopped with just enough mayo to keep it moist and a pinch of sugar to offset the bold flavors in the accompanying BBQ. **SERVES 8**

INGREDIENTS

- ¾ cup mayonnaise
- ¼ cup white vinegar
- ¼ cup sugar
- Seasoning salt, to taste
- Freshly ground black pepper, to taste
- 4 cups green cabbage, finely chopped
- ½ cup carrot, finely chopped
- 2 tablespoons fresh parsley, finely chopped
- 4 tablespoons scallions, finely chopped

METHOD

In a large bowl, whisk together mayonnaise, vinegar, sugar, salt, and pepper. Add cabbage, carrot, parsley, and scallions; toss to combine. Refrigerate until ready to serve.

TIP

To help produce a consistent size and to save time, use a food processor to chop your vegetables.

FRIED OKRA

THERE'S A GOOD REASON this is often referred to as Southern Popcorn. Once you start eating fried okra, it's hard to stop. **SERVES 4**

INGREDIENTS

- 2 eggs
- ½ cup buttermilk
- 1 tablespoon chipotle pepper, minced (about 1 pepper from 7-ounce can with adobo sauce)
- 1 cup all-purpose flour
- 1 cup cornmeal
- 1 tablespoon pepper
- 1 tablespoon kosher salt
- 2 teaspoons cumin
- Canola oil
- 1 pound okra, washed, stemmed, and cut into ½-inch pieces

METHOD

In a small bowl, beat eggs, whisk in buttermilk, and add chipotle pepper. In a second bowl, mix flour, cornmeal, pepper, salt, and cumin.

Add about 1 inch of canola oil to frying pan and heat to medium high (about 350°F).

Working in batches of about ¼ pound of okra at a time, first soak the okra in the egg mix, then dredge in flour, shaking off excess before dropping gently into the hot oil. Fry until golden brown and place on paper towels to remove oil before serving.

COLLARD GREENS WITH HAM

THROUGHOUT THE SOUTH there are as many variations of collard recipes as there are backyard collard patches. Unfortunately, most result in a tough and bitter end product, compromising this otherwise flavorful vegetable.

I learned a couple of tricks that help eliminate the bitterness and produce wonderful greens. First, get rid of the water used to boil the greens; that's what holds all the bitterness. Second, lean on some old faithfuls in classic Southern cooking—smoked ham, sugar, and lard—to create a depth of rich flavors. Don't worry, we've been eating lard for years and seem to still be kicking just fine. **SERVES 8**

INGREDIENTS

40 ounces collard greens (about 2 bunches), washed, stemmed, and roughly chopped into 2- to 3-inch pieces

2½ tablespoons coarse salt, divided

4 tablespoons lard

1½ cups smoked ham, cubed

1 large Vidalia or other sweet onion, diced

3 cloves garlic, diced

3¼ cups chicken broth

¼ cup apple cider vinegar

8 teaspoons sugar

½ teaspoon black pepper

METHOD

Fill large saucepan or stockpot with 7 to 8 quarts water. Place collard greens and 2 tablespoons salt in water and bring to boil. Lower heat to simmer and cook 20 to 25 minutes, until collards are soft.

Discard cooking water and strain collard greens completely. Once greens are cool enough to handle, squeeze dry in small batches and place on a cutting board. Chop/slice each batch 5 or 6 times. Wash and dry pot for use in balance of recipe.

Melt lard in clean pot. Add ham and onion and sauté on medium heat until ham browns, about 5 minutes. Add garlic and continue cooking for about 2 minutes.

Add chicken broth, vinegar, sugar, remaining salt, and pepper to ham mixture. Bring to boil. Add chopped collard greens and return to boil.

Lower heat and adjust seasonings to taste. Cook 5 minutes and serve.

TIP

Collard greens vary widely by season. During colder months, they tend to be sweeter than in the summer. Don't be afraid to increase the sugar to help make your greens turn out just right.

CORNBREAD SALAD

MONICA AND I ENJOY visiting small towns searching for "treasures" in old hardware and antique stores. We never know what we'll discover, but it's certain we'll unearth something that most always ends up in one of my restaurants. We were in Gonzales, Texas, when I came across an old cowboy cookbook that had a recipe for a sweet pickle salad dressing that caught my eye. I played around with it until I came up with a blend of this sweet and savory dressing that has been a customer favorite since we opened the first Smokehouse in 2009. You can use any kind of cornbread, but I'm partial to Jiffy (the blue box) because of its extra sweet flavor. **SERVES 8**

INGREDIENTS

¾ cup mayonnaise

¼ cup bread-and-butter pickle juice

1 pound tomatoes, diced

1 large red bell pepper, diced

1 large yellow bell pepper, diced

1 cup bread-and-butter pickles, chopped

1 cup Vidalia onion, diced

2 pounds romaine lettuce, coarsely chopped

Coarse salt and freshly ground black pepper

4 cups crumbled cornbread

¼ cup crumbled bacon

METHOD

Whisk together mayonnaise and pickle juice in a small bowl; set aside.

Combine tomatoes, red and yellow peppers, pickles, and onion in a large bowl and season with salt and pepper to taste.

Fold mayonnaise mixture into tomato mixture. Dressing is best if made and refrigerated a day before serving to allow the flavors to mature.

Place lettuce in a separate large bowl; top with ¾ of the tomato mixture and toss gently to coat lettuce.

Top with remaining ¼ dressing, then cornbread, and lastly with bacon.

SMOKEHOUSE CORN

JEFF PALERMO CREATED this dish while making dinner for his wife, Meredith, when he wanted something fresh and light to complement grilled chicken. Charring the ears of corn on the grill releases the sugar in the kernels and provides a touch of smoky flavor. This has always been one of our most popular dishes at the Smokehouse.

SERVES 8 TO 10

INGREDIENTS

12 dozen ears fresh corn, or two 16-ounce bags frozen sweet corn

½ cup scallions, white part only

⅓ cup olive oil

1 clove garlic, finely minced

¼ cup scallions, green part only

Coarse salt and freshly ground black pepper, to taste

1 can Rotel Original diced tomatoes and green chilies

⅓ cup chopped cilantro

METHOD

Shuck corn and shear off kernels with a sharp knife over a bowl; set aside. Discard cobs.

Sauté scallion whites in olive oil in a large skillet over medium-high heat. Reduce heat, stir in garlic, and sauté for 2 minutes, being careful not to brown. Add scallion tops and sauté for 1 minute.

Stir in corn and cook for 8 to 10 minutes, or until heated through. Season with salt and pepper.

Add Rotel tomatoes and simmer for 10 minutes.

Stir in cilantro; adjust seasoning to taste. Serve hot.

TIP

Add a couple of tablespoons of sugar while simmering if your corn isn't quite sweet enough.

SOUPS, SIDES, AND SALADS

BIG DOG CHILI

MY FIRST "PUBLIC FEEDING" was in 1999 when John's Big Dog Chili Team came to life to compete in a chili contest benefiting United Cerebral Palsy. Though our empty beer can pyramid generated more comments than our chili, we had a great time and the experience lit a fire that ultimately led to a winning recipe. It took a few years, but we finally started bringing home trophies ... as well as pictures of some pretty cool beer pyramids. **MAKES 15 (1-CUP) SERVINGS**

BIG DOG CHILI

3 dried red chili peppers

1 pound ground breakfast sausage

2 tablespoons vegetable oil

1 pound 80-20 ground beef, coarse or chili grind

4 cups Vidalia onion, chopped

1 cup fresh Anaheim pepper, diced and seeds removed

2 tablespoons fresh garlic, minced

7½ tablespoons chili powder (Gebhardt preferred)

1 tablespoon hot chili powder (Gebhardt preferred)

3½ pounds chopped smoked beef brisket, lean cut

2 cups beef broth

½ tablespoon dried oregano

¼ cup cumin

1½ cups tomato sauce

2 cups Rotel Original chopped tomatoes

2 cups chicken stock

1 cup corn tortilla chips, crushed

½ tablespoon cayenne

1½ tablespoons brown sugar

ACCOMPANIMENTS

Fritos corn chips

Cheddar cheese, shredded

Corn bread

Sour cream

Pickled jalapeños

Hot sauce

METHOD

Add dried peppers to 1 cup water in a small saucepan. Bring to a boil, then reduce heat to simmer for about 30 minutes, or until peppers are soft. Remove stems and puree in a blender with 2 tablespoons of liquid from pan. Set aside.

Brown sausage in vegetable oil in a large stockpot over medium heat. Remove meat with slotted spoon and set aside. Add ground beef and brown; remove with slotted spoon and set aside. In same pan, sauté onion and Anaheim peppers for 3 minutes. Add garlic and continue to sauté until onion is translucent, taking care not to brown the garlic.

Combine chili powders in a small bowl.

Add brisket to stockpot with half of chili powder mix; cook for 15 minutes. Add beef broth, oregano, and cumin; cook for 15 minutes. Stir in tomato sauce, Rotel tomatoes, and dried-chili puree and continue to simmer for 15 minutes.

Stir in cooked ground beef, sausage, remaining chili powder, chicken stock, and crushed tortilla chips. Cook over medium heat for 15 to 20 minutes. Stir in cayenne, brown sugar, and a pinch of cumin just before serving.

To serve, spoon chili over a handful of Fritos in a bowl, then top with cheddar cheese, crumbled corn bread, a dollop of sour cream, pickled jalapeños, and a dash of hot sauce.

FRITO CHILI PIE

MONICA GREW UP eating chili in Fritos bags at her high school's football games on cold Texas nights. Frito Chili Pie is more a conversation piece than a pie, but it sure is a fun way to enjoy chili at a tailgate party. I'm including the directions for assembly in case you get the opportunity to give it a try. **1 SERVING**

INGREDIENTS

1 (2-ounce) bag Fritos or other corn chips

1 cup Big Dog Chili

2 tablespoons cheddar cheese, shredded

1 tablespoon sour cream

2 slices fresh jalapeños

METHOD

Cut open front of chip bag and peel back to create a bowl-like opening. Place bag in a paper banana boat or long bowl. Spoon chili onto chips in bag; top with cheese, sour cream, and jalapeño slices.

SOUPS, SIDES, AND SALADS

CILANTRO POTATO SALAD

THIS IS A DISH that I'm convinced has a different version for just about every region and every ethnicity in the country. It truly is one that you like the version closest to what you grew up eating. My mom could make some mean potato salad, and that's where this recipe originated. I updated hers by substituting Creole mustard for yellow, and adding a touch of sugar, a splash of pickle juice, and a handful of cilantro. The rest I left to dear old Mom. **SERVES 8**

INGREDIENTS

3 pounds red-skinned potatoes, quartered

2 teaspoons extra-virgin olive oil

2 teaspoons kosher salt

½ teaspoon sugar

½ teaspoon freshly ground black pepper

Dash hot sauce

¾ cup mayonnaise

½ cup dill pickles, chopped

½ cup sweet onion, diced

½ cup fresh cilantro leaves, chopped

¼ cup green onion, chopped

2 tablespoons Creole mustard

2 tablespoons dill pickle juice

2 hard-boiled eggs, peeled and chopped

METHOD

Boil potatoes in salted water for about 15 minutes, or until fork-tender. Drain, rinse in cold water, and then set aside to cool.

Transfer potatoes to a large bowl and lightly drizzle with olive oil. Sprinkle with salt, sugar, pepper, and hot sauce. Toss lightly to coat, being careful not to smash potatoes.

Combine mayonnaise, pickles, sweet onion, cilantro, green onion, mustard, pickle juice, and hard-boiled eggs. Stir until thoroughly mixed. Pour dressing over potatoes and toss gently until well coated.

Cover and refrigerate at least 2 hours or overnight. Can be made 2 or 3 days in advance.

John's mom, Teresa Nolan and Monica's, Jeanette Henke

SOUPS, SIDES, AND SALADS

BAKED CHEESE GRITS

INSPIRED BY PAULA DEEN'S recipe, the vibrant yellow and "cornbread-like" presentation of an otherwise unattractive white and runny side dish is enough to make even the most stubborn Northerner fall in love with this Southern delight. The cheese adds color and silkiness, while baking it allows you the ability to cut and shape the grits for a more creative and appealing presentation.
SERVES 10 TO 12

INGREDIENTS

4 cups chicken broth

1 teaspoon coarse salt

1 teaspoon black pepper

1 cup yellow stone-ground grits (I prefer Anson Mills)

½ cup cheddar cheese

4 ounces (6 slices) Velveeta cheese

2 tablespoons butter

½ teaspoon garlic powder

2 large eggs

¼ cup milk

TIP

Add the salt and pepper before boiling to allow the grits to absorb the flavor. For creamier grits, substitute one-fourth of the chicken broth with cream or half-and-half.

METHOD

Preheat oven to 325°F.

Bring chicken broth, salt, and pepper to a boil in a medium saucepan over medium-high heat.

Stir in grits, reduce heat to simmer, cover pan, and cook 15 minutes, or until broth is absorbed, whisking occasionally. Remove from heat.

Add cheddar, Velveeta, butter, and garlic powder, stirring until cheeses are melted. Set aside.

Beat eggs lightly in a small bowl. Whisk a small amount of eggs into hot grits, mixing well. Gradually whisk remaining eggs into grits, whisking continuously. Whisk in milk.

Pour into greased 8-inch-square baking dish. Bake 30 minutes. Let stand at least 20 minutes before serving.

OPTIONAL

To serve in a specific shape, cover and refrigerate until cooled. Cut in desired shape in pan and warm in oven on low heat before serving.

SOUPS, SIDES, AND SALADS

COLLARD-INFUSED BAKED CHEESE GRITS

THOUGH RELATIVELY FLAVORLESS on their own, grits provide a wonderfully versatile foundation upon which to combine flavors. One fun experiment we tried was adding wine to the cheese grits for a wine and cheese party. Exhaustive R & D was necessary to identify the perfect wine and cheese pairing, but that goes with the job.

My favorite combination comes from bittersweet collard greens against the smoky undertones of pork and the sharp saltiness of cheddar cheese. It's a delicious way to dress up a plate while maintaining the Southern integrity of the otherwise simple grits. **SERVES 6**

INGREDIENTS

1 cup Collard Greens with Ham, drained (page 59)

4 cups unbaked Cheese Grits (facing page, steps 1-5 only)

1 tablespoon hot sauce, such as Crystal or Texas Pete

¼ teaspoon garlic, chopped

METHOD

Preheat oven to 325°F.

Stir together all ingredients in a mixing bowl.

Pour into an 8-by-8-inch ovenproof dish and bake for 25 minutes, or until set.

Serve hot or, if shaping, cover and refrigerate until cooled.

Cut with desired shape mold (such as a biscuit cutter), place on a baking sheet, and reheat at 225°F for 20 minutes before serving.

PHOTO BY MICHAEL PISARRI

MARTHA'S BRUNSWICK STEW

WHILE DEBATE ENDURES over exactly where Brunswick stew originated—some claim it has roots in Virginia's Brunswick County, while others hold it comes from Brunswick, Georgia—there's no arguing that it is beloved throughout the South. This particular recipe, which plays off the earthiness of our smoked meats and tomatoes, comes from our friend Martha Burn, a member of our original team at the Smokehouse and, to further complicate the origin story, a South Carolina native. **SERVES 10 TO 12**

INGREDIENTS

¾ pound sage-flavored pork breakfast sausage

2 tablespoons salted butter

2 cups Vidalia onion, diced

1 cup celery, diced

3 tablespoons garlic, chopped

4 cups grilled corn kernels

4 cups chopped smoked tomatoes

6 cups chicken stock

3 cups potato, diced

¾ cup Worcestershire sauce

¾ cup All-Purpose BBQ Sauce (page 25)

2 large bay leaves

1 tablespoon dried oregano

½ tablespoon granulated garlic

½ tablespoon ground allspice

1 teaspoon freshly ground black pepper

2 cups fresh or frozen lima beans

4 cups pulled smoked chicken (approximately 1 pound)

3 cups cubed smoked brisket (approximately ½ pound)

2 tablespoons fresh basil, roughly chopped

METHOD

Heat a large stockpot over medium-high heat. Add sausage and cook until golden brown, breaking sausage into bite-size pieces. Remove sausage with a slotted spoon and transfer to a plate; set aside.

Add butter to sausage renderings in stockpot. Add onions and sauté 2 minutes. Add celery and sauté 2 minutes more. Add garlic and sauté until fragrant, about 1 minute, then add corn. Cook, stirring, until vegetables are golden. Add tomatoes, stirring to combine. Simmer 1 minute. Add chicken stock and potatoes, stirring to combine. Cover and simmer 15 minutes.

Stir in Worcestershire, BBQ sauce, bay leaves, oregano, granulated garlic, allspice, and pepper. Add lima beans and simmer, covered, 5 minutes more. Uncover and gently stir in chicken, brisket, and reserved sausage. Simmer, uncovered, 10 minutes, or until thick.

Just before serving, stir in fresh basil.

Note: For smoked tomatoes, follow first 2 paragraphs of method for Smoked Tomato Jam (page 48). Or, you may substitute canned fire-roasted tomatoes.

BREADS AND BREAKFAST

★

SHRIMP AND GRITS

ONE SIDE OF MY family hails from Charleston, South Carolina, where shrimp and grits is the de facto representative of the region's low-country cooking style. Shrimp and grits can be served for breakfast, lunch, or dinner. Although there are many variations of the recipe, the core flavors include pork-laced, thin tomato sauce with just a hint of heat over creamy grits. My favorite recipe comes from S.N.O.B. (Slightly North of Broad), located in the heart of downtown Charleston. They graciously shared their recipe, and I played around with it to come up with my variation of the classic.

The key to shrimp and grits lies as much in the quality of the grits as the freshness of the shrimp. Splurge on high-quality, stone-ground grits, like those from Anson Mills, and you won't regret it.

SERVES 4

SHRIMP STOCK

1 pound fresh medium shrimp (approximately 25-30)

1 tablespoon olive oil

2 stalks celery with leaves, thinly sliced

½ medium onion, thinly sliced

½ teaspoon crushed red pepper flakes

½ teaspoon freshly ground black pepper

8 ounces tomato paste

3 quarts cold water

GRITS

1¼ cups stone-ground yellow grits

4 cups shrimp stock

1 tablespoon unsalted butter

½ teaspoon coarse salt

½ teaspoon freshly ground black pepper

¼ cup heavy cream

SHRIMP

2 tablespoons unsalted butter, divided

4 ounces tasso, diced (can substitute prosciutto or smoked ham)

1 (4-ounce) link andouille sausage, diced

1 teaspoon garlic, chopped

¼ teaspoon cayenne

½ cup diced tomato

¼ cup sliced green onion (green tops only)

½ cup chicken stock

ACCOMPANIMENT

Hot sauce

CONTINUED

BREADS AND BREAKFAST

MAKE SHRIMP STOCK

If shrimp are frozen, place in a colander set over a bowl in the refrigerator and thaw overnight. Save all liquid that thaws from shrimp.

Peel shrimp, including tails, reserving shells. Butterfly shrimp and remove impurities; set shrimp aside in refrigerator until ready to use.

Heat olive oil in a heavy stockpot over medium-high heat; add reserved shrimp shells. Stir occasionally until all shells are pink and, in places, golden.

Add celery, onion, red pepper flakes, and black pepper. Sauté until vegetables are softened, about 8 minutes.

Add tomato paste and stir in until it coats the shells and vegetables. Add reserved juices from thawing shrimp and water; turn heat to high and bring to boil. Reduce heat and maintain low simmer for 1 hour.

Strain stock through a fine-mesh sieve, crushing all the liquid from the shells and vegetables using a wooden spoon. Set stock aside.

MAKE GRITS

Rinse grits in a large bowl of water, removing any bran or hulls that float to the surface. Drain well.

Combine shrimp stock, butter, salt, and pepper in a medium saucepan over high heat and bring to a boil. Whisk in grits. Turn heat to low and simmer 30 to 40 minutes, stirring occasionally.

Remove from heat and stir in cream. Keep warm.

MAKE SHRIMP

Heat 1 tablespoon butter in a large sauté pan over medium-high heat. Add shrimp and cook 1 to 2 minutes, until they are just cooked through. Remove shrimp from sauté pan and set aside.

In the same pan, add tasso and andouille and cook 3 to 4 minutes, or until golden.

Add garlic and cayenne, stirring to combine. Add tomato and green onion and sauté 30 seconds.

Return shrimp to pan; add chicken stock and simmer 1 to 2 minutes, or until slightly reduced. Swirl in remaining 1 tablespoon of butter.

ASSEMBLE

Divide grits among 4 serving bowls and add a portion of shrimp mixture to each serving. Top with a splash of hot sauce.

TIP

A secret to making good grits is to use a stock (chicken, shrimp, fish) and a touch of heavy cream to boil the grits, versus just using water. Doing so results in creamier grits with a nice depth and balance of flavor.

SKILLET CORNBREAD

WHEN WE SAY "SKILLET" we really mean cast-iron skillet. You can cook it in a different type of pan, but only the distribution and intensity of heat from cast iron will give this cornbread the desired crispy crust while keeping it soft and moist inside. It's worth the effort and expense to use a cast-iron skillet if you can. **MAKES 1 (10-INCH) ROUND**

INGREDIENTS

½ pound bacon, chopped

¾ cup sifted all-purpose flour

1¼ cups cornmeal

½ cup grilled corn, finely chopped

½ cup sugar

2 teaspoons baking powder

1 teaspoon salt

½ teaspoon baking soda

1 cup buttermilk

1 cup butter, melted

⅓ cup whole milk

2 eggs, lightly beaten

1 cup cheddar cheese, shredded

2 tablespoons sliced scallions

1 tablespoon chopped fresh cilantro

Salted butter, as needed

METHOD

Preheat oven to 400°F.

Cook bacon in a 10-inch cast-iron skillet over medium heat until crisp. Remove all pieces and debris of bacon from pan with a slotted spoon and transfer to a plate lined with paper towels; leave bacon grease in skillet.

Place skillet in oven to preheat for 10 minutes or more.

In a large bowl, combine sifted flour, cornmeal, corn, sugar, baking powder, salt, and baking soda; stir to mix.

In a medium bowl, whisk together buttermilk, butter, milk, and eggs; add to dry ingredients, stirring until just combined. Do not overstir.

Add cheddar, scallions, and cilantro and stir to combine.

Carefully remove skillet from oven. Rotate skillet so remaining bacon grease is equally distributed on bottom and sides of skillet. Add butter as needed to assure grease covers the entire skillet bottom and sides. Pour batter into hot skillet and smooth top with a rubber spatula. Batter will sizzle when it hits the skillet.

Return hot skillet to oven and bake until cornbread is golden brown and center springs back when lightly pressed, 20 to 25 minutes.

> **TIP**
>
> The key to this cornbread is making sure the bacon grease is hot before you pour in the batter. Don't worry if it begins to smoke a little in the oven; it's all for the better.

KOLACHES

FEW QUESTIONS ELICIT a more fervent debate than asking Texans to name the best style of kolache. Relatively unknown in the U.S. beyond the Lone Star State, this delectable pastry rapidly grew in popularity after being introduced by the large numbers of Czechoslovakian immigrants who settled in Central Texas between Austin and Dallas in the late 1800s. Kolache festivals take place throughout the state, with young women competing for the coveted title of "Kolache Queen." While I appreciate the traditional fruit-filled kolaches, the savory Texas twist of stuffing it with sausage, cheese, and jalapeños is my favorite. I can't imagine what led someone to do that, but I for one am thankful for the indulgent take on the Czech classic. **MAKES 16**

KOLACHE DOUGH

4 to 4½ cups all-purpose flour, divided

1 cup whole milk

¼ cup sugar

1 package active dry yeast

½ cup vegetable oil

2 eggs, separated

1 teaspoon salt

½ stick butter, melted

FRUIT AND CREAM CHEESE FILLINGS

2 cups fruit (such as blueberries, chopped strawberries, or diced apple)

1 cup sugar, divided

⅓ cup light brown sugar

½ cup apple juice concentrate

8 ounces cream cheese, softened

1 large egg

1 teaspoon vanilla extract

CRUMB TOPPING

½ cup sugar

½ cup flour

¼ cup cold butter, cubed

MAKE DOUGH

Combine milk and sugar in a medium saucepan over medium heat; heat until barely simmering, then remove from heat.

Sprinkle yeast over milk mixture and lightly stir with a fork until yeast dissolves. Set aside for 5 to 8 minutes, until bubbles form on surface.

Pour milk mixture over 2 cups flour in a large bowl and fold together until completely combined. Cover loosely with a clean kitchen towel and set aside until mixture doubles in size, about 20 minutes.

Combine oil, egg yolks, and salt in a medium bowl, whisking to combine. Stir into dough.

Whip egg whites with an electric mixer until stiff peaks form; gently fold into dough.

Add remaining 2 to 2½ cups flour to dough, ½ cup at a time, until dough is pliable and no longer very sticky.

Portion dough into 1-inch balls.

Place on a greased sheet pan with only ½ inch separating each ball in a "crowded" fashion so that the edge of each rises and bakes up against the next. Doing so creates uniformity in the shape and assists in creating a taller pastry.

Brush tops with melted butter.

Wrap pan with plastic wrap and refrigerate overnight.

MAKE FRUIT AND CREAM CHEESE FILLINGS

Combine fruit, ¾ cup sugar, brown sugar, and apple juice concentrate in a medium saucepan over medium-high heat. Bring to a boil, then reduce to a simmer and cook until mixture thickens, about 15 to 20 minutes.

Set aside to cool completely.

Combine cream cheese, remaining ¼ cup sugar, egg, and vanilla extract in a small bowl, whisking well until completely combined.

MAKE CRUMB TOPPING

Combine sugar and flour in a medium bowl.

Place butter in flour mixture and break apart with fingers until pea-size crumbs form.

ASSEMBLE

Make an indention in the center of each piece of dough using fingers or the back of a spoon. Fill indentation with 1 tablespoon cream cheese and 1 tablespoon fruit filling. Sprinkle crumb-topping mixture heavily on top.

Preheat oven to 350°F. While oven preheats, place pan of kolaches on top of stove to rise for 10 minutes. Bake 25 minutes, or until golden brown. Brush with additional melted butter, if desired, when kolaches come out of oven.

KOLACHES
SAUSAGE, CHEESE, AND JALAPEÑO VARIATION

INGREDIENTS

Melted butter, for brushing

1 (8-ounce) block cheddar cheese cut into 16 long rectangles

½ cup jalapeños, chopped

½ pound smoked sausage links, cut into 16 long rectangles

METHOD

Lightly flour a clean countertop or table. Place one dough ball on surface. Make an indentation using 2 fingers down center of dough to form a rectangle.

Brush with melted butter. Place a piece of cheese in center.

Sprinkle jalapeños down center of cheese, reserving some for garnish. Place sausage, cut side up, on top. Fold short ends up over edges of sausage.

Fold one long end halfway up, and cover with opposite end.

Pinch seams together and shape dough in your hand to form a smooth cylinder.

Place on a greased sheet pan with only ½ inch separating each kolache in a "crowded" fashion so that the edge of each rises and bakes up against the next. Doing so creates uniformity in the shape and assists in creating a taller pastry.

Brush tops with melted butter and a few chopped jalapeños. Place on top of oven and let rise until doubled.

Bake at 350°F until golden brown, about 25 minutes. Brush with melted butter after removing from oven.

GRUYÈRE HERB BISCUITS

A GRATEFUL NOD to my friend Julie Petrakis, chef and cofounder of the Ravenous Pig in Winter Park, who inspired this recipe with her own version of Gruyère biscuits. I developed this recipe in response to the need for a unique bread option to accompany our Coffee-Rubbed Cowboy Rib Eye (page 130) at a pop-up kitchen event. We fell in love with the silky-savory flavor resulting from combining the herbs and Gruyère with copious amounts of butter to create a light, yet flavor-rich, biscuit.

MAKES 16 TO 18 BISCUITS

INGREDIENTS

2¼ cups all-purpose flour

2 teaspoons baking powder

½ teaspoon baking soda

1 teaspoon table salt

1½ sticks unsalted butter, cut in ½-inch cubes and chilled

1 teaspoon fresh thyme, finely chopped

½ teaspoon fresh sage, finely chopped

1 cup Gruyère cheese, shredded and chilled

1 cup buttermilk

2 tablespoons unsalted butter, melted

2 tablespoons coarse, flaky salt

METHOD

Preheat oven to 425°F.

Whisk together flour, baking powder, baking soda, and table salt in a large mixing bowl.

Add chilled butter and cut into flour with a pastry blender or food processor until a mixture of fine crumbs (some pea-size) form. If using a food processor, combine in 2 batches and do not over-process. Only a couple of pulses are needed. Return to mixing bowl.

Add thyme, sage, and cheese.

Stir in buttermilk until dough is moist. Add a very small amount of extra buttermilk, if necessary, to reach desired consistency.

Sprinkle flour over a flat working surface and place dough in center of it. Rubbing flour on your rolling pin as well, flatten and knead dough 3-4 times into a ½-inch-thick rectangle.

On the fourth knead, place thinly sliced pats of cold butter on the upper second ¼ of the dough and fold the top fourth over it. Layer a second row of butter on the 3rd section of the dough in a manner to avoid stacking the butter directly above the first row and fold the larger section over the butter. Place a final row of butter pats on top of the folded sections and fold the remaining ¼ over to cover. As the dough bakes, the butter will expand and create distinct and fluffy layers. Make sure the dough is chilled when you place it in the oven or else the biscuits will get hot pockets and not be as fluffy.

Cut dough into approximately 2-by-2-inch squares and place on a greased baking sheet, leaving 1 inch between biscuits. Cover and refrigerate for at least 20 minutes or up to an hour.

Remove from refrigerator. Brush with melted butter and sprinkle with flaky salt, to taste. Bake 20 minutes or until lightly golden. Serve hot.

COWBOY SKILLET SCRAMBLE

PERHAPS BECAUSE IT'S the only meal we're able to enjoy while still in pajamas, breakfast has always been my favorite to cook. The sound of bacon sizzling and the aroma of fresh coffee brewing conjures memories of growing up that I keep close to my heart.

This particular dish has been my go-to when feeding a large crew. The vibrant reds and greens of the tomatoes and scallions pop against the yellow of the fluffy eggs and the dark colors of the bacon and sausage. Serve with some warm tortillas and fresh salsa, and you'll be the hero of the pajama party. **SERVES UP TO 20**

INGREDIENTS

3 dozen flour tortillas

3 dozen eggs, beaten

2 tablespoons whole milk

Salt and pepper to taste

½ cup fresh cilantro, roughly chopped, divided

1 pound cheddar cheese, shredded, divided

Few dashes hot sauce

3 pounds hickory smoked bacon, diced

2 pounds crumbled breakfast, wild boar, or chorizo sausage

4 cups scallions, chopped, green part only

1 fresh jalapeño, seeds and stem removed to decrease heat, diced

3 tablespoons butter

4 Roma tomatoes, diced

3 whole jalapeños for garnish

1 bottle store-bought salsa or Pico de Gallo (page 33)

METHOD

Grill tortillas until slightly brown, wrap in foil, and set aside to keep warm. If a grill isn't available, stack tortillas in the center of a sheet of foil, a dozen at a time, lay a damp paper towel over the top tortilla, and wrap tight. Place in oven and bake at 225°F for 20 minutes to warm. Remove from oven and keep warm and wrapped in foil until ready to serve. Repeat for remaining tortillas, a dozen at a time in a foil pack.

Whisk eggs with milk, salt, pepper, ½ of the cilantro, ½ of the cheese, and hot sauce. Set aside.

In a 20-inch skillet, fry bacon and set aside to drain on paper towels. Repeat with sausage. Leave grease in skillet.

Add scallions and jalapeños to skillet and sauté until just softened. Remove, drain pan, and wipe clean with a paper towel.

Melt butter over medium-high heat. Add eggs and allow to sit for 30 seconds before gently stirring once. Allow to sit for another 30 seconds. Reduce heat to low and gently stir until eggs are soft scrambled but runny. Remove from heat and continue to gently scramble for a couple of minutes.

Push scrambled eggs to the center of the skillet, leaving a 2-inch ring around the outside of the eggs. Spoon sausage around eggs in the open ring.

Leaving a 2-inch exposed outer ring of eggs, sprinkle bacon in a circle on top of remaining eggs. Fill the inside of the bacon ring with chopped tomatoes. Place onions and jalapeños on top of the tomatoes in a smaller circle. Garnish with whole jalapeños.

Serve with warm tortillas, shredded cheese, salsa or pico de gallo, and remaining cilantro.

MIGAS BREAKFAST TORTILLAS

I DISCOVERED THIS Tex-Mex-flavored dish (pronounced "mee-yas") in a quaint Central Texas diner when I mistakenly ordered it thinking it was huevos rancheros. Originating in Spain and Portugal, the traditional version of *migas* (meaning "crumbs" in English) is a soup made from leftover tortillas and bread. How it became a breakfast scramble with chorizo is a mystery likely linked back to some gringo. The distinct corn flavor of the tortilla pairs well against the fresh pop of the cilantro and the subtle heat of the jalapeño. Excellent served with refried beans and a spicy Bloody Mary to start the day. **SERVES UP TO 4**

INGREDIENTS

1 large or 2 small poblano peppers, stems removed

12 (6-inch) flour tortillas

¼ pound smoked brisket, chicken or pork, or uncooked chorizo, chopped

1 dozen eggs, beaten

1 tablespoon half-and-half

Salt and pepper to taste

½ cup fresh cilantro, roughly chopped, divided

1½ cups cheddar, mozzarella, Colby, or Monterey Jack cheese, shredded, divided

Few dashes hot sauce

2 tablespoons butter

1 medium Vidalia onion, finely chopped

1 fresh jalapeño, seeds and stem removed to decrease heat, diced, divided

3 (6-inch) corn tortillas, torn or cut into 1-inch pieces

1 medium tomato, diced

1 jar store-bought salsa or Pico de Gallo (page 33)

METHOD

Grill poblano on all sides until outer skin is blackened. This can be done over an open flame of a gas grill or broiled in the oven. Place charred pepper in a brown paper bag, close bag, and allow to sit unopened for 20 minutes for the skin to separate or "sweat" from the pepper.

While the poblano is sweating in the bag, grill 12 flour tortillas until slightly brown; wrap in foil and set aside to keep warm. If a grill isn't available, lay tortillas in the center of a sheet of foil; lay a damp paper towel over the top tortilla and wrap tightly in the foil. Place in oven and bake at 200°F for 20 minutes to warm. Remove from oven and keep warm and wrapped in foil until ready to serve.

Remove pepper from bag. Slice one side vertically from tip to bottom, remove seeds, and lay on a flat surface in one whole piece with the charred side up. Using the flat side of a knife, scrape the charred skin off, leaving the bright green flesh of the pepper exposed. Cut into thin 1-inch strips and set aside.

If adding chorizo or any other uncooked meat, sauté until done (or warmed) and set aside on paper towel to drain. Wipe skillet clean, once cooled.

Whisk eggs thoroughly. Add half-and-half, salt and pepper, ½ of the cilantro, 1 cup of the cheese, and hot sauce. Mix to combine and set aside.

Melt butter in a nonstick skillet over medium-high heat. Add onion, poblanos, and ½ of the jalapeño. Sauté until onions just begin to sweat (2 minutes). Add corn tortilla pieces, tomato, and meat, and continue sautéing until onions are translucent (3 to 4 minutes).

Reduce heat to medium-low, add eggs, and begin a slow, soft scramble, pulling from the outer rim of the eggs and folding in toward the middle. Continue the soft scramble, folding in toward the center all the while, until eggs are firm but still shiny (runny).

Remove from heat, add ½ of the cilantro (saving some for garnish), and remaining ½ cup of shredded cheese, and continue the soft folding scramble for another 30 seconds or until eggs reach desired stiffness. Transfer eggs onto a serving platter immediately (or they will continue to cook in the hot skillet).

Spoon 2 big scoops of egg scramble onto a warm flour tortilla. Top with cilantro, jalapeños, pico de gallo, and more cheese, if desired. Fold tortilla around eggs and serve warm.

BREADS AND BREAKFAST

SANDWICHES

GRILLED HAM MAC AND CHEESE

IN A WORD: DECADENT. This over-the-top creation was a result of my affinity for putting potato chips inside sandwiches as a child and my daughter Cameron's infatuation with mac and cheese. What better way to marry the two than combining it with another childhood favorite, the traditional grilled cheese sandwich. Don't be scared of the jalapeños. They provide more of a balance of flavors than heat. **MAKES 1 SANDWICH**

INGREDIENTS

2 eggs

3 tablespoons mayonnaise, divided

2 thick slices (¾ inch) challah bread

4 ounces or 2 to 3 slices Velveeta cheese

3 thin slices ham

6 pickled jalapeño slices

¼ cup cold macaroni and cheese, made from your favorite recipe

¼ cup crushed ridged potato chips

3 tablespoons butter, melted

Hot sauce to taste

METHOD

Whisk eggs and 1 tablespoon mayonnaise in a small bowl to make an egg wash; set aside. Heat a cast-iron skillet or griddle to medium-hot.

Spread inside of both slices of challah with remaining mayonnaise. Layer cheese, ham, jalapeños, and macaroni and cheese, then place remaining bread on top.

Brush sandwich on both sides with egg wash; coat with potato chips and press chips down gently to assure they're set in bread. Brush one side of sandwich with melted butter and place in skillet or on griddle, butter side down. Grill, pressing flat with a spatula, until bottom is golden brown and cheese is melted, 3 to 5 minutes. Brush top with butter, flip, and repeat.

Cut in half diagonally and serve hot along with a bottle of hot sauce to spice to taste.

Cameron and Dad

THE LONGHORN

A GUEST AT THE Smokehouse told us how his father combined our brisket and sausage on a custom-made sandwich at home. It sounded pretty darn good, so we went to work on it. The combination of the pork and beef flavors proved a winner and in true Smokehouse fashion we topped it with fried onion rings and provolone. And since the father was a University of Texas graduate, it only seemed appropriate to call it the Longhorn. **MAKES 1 SANDWICH**

INGREDIENTS

2 tablespoons dill pickles, chopped

1 tablespoon pickled jalapeños, chopped

1 medium hoagie bun

Butter

2 ounces All-Purpose BBQ Sauce (page 25)

½ cup cooked smoked sausage, chopped

½ cup Smoked Brisket (page 116), chopped

2 fried onion rings, made from your favorite recipe

1½ slices provolone cheese

METHOD

Stir together dill pickles and pickled jalapeños to make relish. Refrigerate until ready to use.

Preheat oven to 300°F.

Butter hoagie bun and place on a heated griddle or in a large skillet until golden.

Spread pickle-jalapeño relish on bun and top with BBQ sauce.

Combine sausage and brisket and place in bun. Top with onion rings and provolone cheese.

Place in oven until cheese is melted. Serve immediately.

GRILLED CUBAN SANDWICH

ONE OF MY FAVORITE memories of growing up in Florida is fishing with my Uncle Dicky in the Keys. Our trip wouldn't have been complete without Cuban sandwiches from our favorite joint in Little Havana, appropriately marked with bullet holes in the window and a "No English" sign validating its authenticity.

To add a Smokehouse twist to this local favorite, we use smoked pork in place of roasted, and we added a little BBQ sauce to complement the traditional mojo sauce. Topping it with an onion ring admittedly pushes into taboo territory, but honoring the standard mustard and dill pickle toppings, along with pressing the Cuban roll, keeps us out of trouble with the locals.

MAKES 1 (6-INCH) SANDWICH

MOJO SAUCE

¾ cup red wine vinegar

2 tablespoons fresh lemon juice

2 tablespoons fresh orange juice

2 tablespoons sugar

2 teaspoons yellow mustard

1 teaspoon granulated garlic

2 tablespoons dried minced onion

1 teaspoon coarse salt

2 teaspoons freshly ground black pepper

1 tablespoon dried oregano

2 teaspoons dried basil

1 teaspoon crushed red pepper

2 teaspoons fresh minced garlic

1½ cups olive oil

CUBAN SANDWICH

6-inch Cuban roll

1 tablespoon yellow mustard

2 tablespoons All-Puroise BBQ Sauce (page 25)

3 slices dill pickles

3 ounces smoked ham, thinly sliced

2½ ounces pork, thinly sliced

2 onion rings, from your favorite recipe

1½ slices provolone cheese, cut in half

Butter, for grilling

MAKE MOJO SAUCE

Whisk together all ingredients except olive oil in a large bowl. Slowly emulsify or whisk in olive oil until blended. Refrigerate overnight or until ready to use. Can be stored for up to 2 weeks.

Monica's stepfather, Myrl, John and Uncle Dickey with the catch of the day

ASSEMBLE AND COOK SANDWICH

Slice bread horizontally in half. Spread each side with mustard, BBQ sauce, and 1 tablespoon mojo sauce. Layer pickles, ham, pork, onion rings, and cheese. Can be made ahead to this point.

Heat grill to medium-hot (use a sandwich or panini press if a grill isn't available).

Butter one side of the bun and place on grill, buttered side down. Place a small plate atop the sandwich and put something heavy on top of the plate to press the sandwich while grilling (a gallon water jug does the trick). Grill for 3 minutes without moving.

Lift the weight and plate and butter the top of sandwich. Flip and repeat grilling under the plate for another 3 to 4 minutes or until cheese is melted and bread is flat and brown. Serve warm.

MESSY PIG

MY FAVORITE WAY to eat pulled pork is in traditional Carolina style—covered in creamy coleslaw. When I was developing the menu for the Smokehouse, I wanted to highlight this culinary form of art and felt it needed to be big, bold, and completely overboard. Appropriately, it had to have a name that delivered the same impact and, thus, the Messy Pig was born. All was going great until my wife learned of my marketing flash of genius and duly informed me, "no one would ever order something called a Messy Pig." Today, it's one of our top-selling sandwiches.

Monica is usually right about things, but after this she decided to leave the cooking and marketing to me. I have to admit, I get a certain degree of pleasure every time I hear a guest say, "I'll have one of those big Messy Pigs." Pass the napkins! **MAKES 1 SANDWICH**

INGREDIENTS

1 sandwich bun

½ cup Southern Coleslaw, divided (page 57)

⅔ cup Pulled Pork (page 152)

6 dill pickle slices

4 pickled jalapeño slices

3 tablespoons-plus All-Purpose BBQ Sauce (page 25)

METHOD

Cover the bottom of the bun with half of the coleslaw.

Layer with pulled pork and remaining coleslaw.

Top with dill pickles and jalapeños, then drown with BBQ sauce.

The Longwood team putting on the final touches before the grand opening

ST. PADDY'S DAY BRISKET BURGER

I WANTED TO CREATE a burger that deserved to be served at the Smokehouse, so what better place to start than with brisket? While working on the recipe at home, however, I ran out of cheese and had to improvise with the closest thing on hand—Cheez-Its! Turns out, they work as an ideal binder for the brisket and add a great tanginess to the burger.

The Brisket Burger is fine by itself, but we go all out on St. Paddy's Day to dress it up the way my son, Jared, and I found burgers prepared in Flanagan's Irish pub in Park City, Utah. We have no Irish in us whatsoever, but R & D on this unique burger combination gave us a reason to visit Flanagan's again and again. **MAKES 6 BURGERS**

BRISKET BURGER SAUCE
Makes about 2¾ cups

1 cup mayonnaise

¼ cup mustard

½ cup ketchup

½ cup All-Purpose BBQ Sauce (page 25)

BURGERS

2 teaspoons vegetable oil

½ medium onion, finely chopped

1 tablespoon garlic, minced

2 pounds ground brisket

⅔ cup cheese crackers, finely crushed, such as Cheez-Its

¼ cup All-Purpose BBQ Sauce (page 25)

3 tablespoons parsley, finely chopped

1 egg, lightly beaten

1 tablespoon Worcestershire sauce

1 teaspoon coarse salt

1 teaspoon freshly ground black pepper

6 slices Swiss cheese

FOR ASSEMBLY

6 buns

9 ounces corned beef, sliced, warm

2 onions, sliced, grilled or caramelized

6 ounces creamy horseradish sauce (or 1 part mayonnaise plus 1 part horseradish)

½ cup Brisket Burger Sauce

1 tomato, sliced

Bibb lettuce

Dill pickle chips

Dad and Jared

MAKE SAUCE

Mix all ingredients in a small bowl. Refrigerate until ready to use.

MAKE BURGERS

Heat oil in a medium sauté pan over medium heat. Add onion, garlic, and a pinch of salt and pepper, then sauté until onion is translucent, about 5 minutes. Set aside to cool.

Combine ground brisket, crushed cheese crackers, BBQ sauce, parsley, egg, Worcestershire, salt, and pepper in a large bowl; mix until thoroughly combined.

Form mixture into 6 equal patties, taking care not to press the patties too tight while forming into shape.

Refrigerate the patties for 30 minutes, uncovered, allowing them to cool to a consistent temperature all the way through. While patties are cooling, light a grill and allow temperature to reach medium-high.

Place cold patties directly on hot grill; avoid overhandling the patties.

Grill on one side for 3 minutes. Flip only once and continue grilling to desired doneness, about 4 more minutes for medium.

Place cheese slices over burgers in the last minute of cooking.

Remove from grill; tent loosely with foil to allow cheese to melt.

ASSEMBLE

Spread creamy horseradish sauce on the bottom half and Brisket Burger Sauce on the top half of each bun. Place a Brisket Burger on the bottom half of each bun, then top with corned beef and caramelized onions and cap with top bun. Serve immediately with sliced tomatoes, Bibb lettuce, dill pickles, and extra Brisket Burger Sauce.

TEXAS DESTROYER

THE IDEA FOR THIS sandwich came to me in the middle of the night. I bolted up in bed, woke my wife, Monica, and told her about it. Much to my dismay, she didn't share in my enthusiasm for middle-of-the-night epiphany. Regardless, it turned out to be a great sandwich that features our smoked brisket along with some other favorite flavors—jalapeños, onion rings, and melted cheese. Though Monica never grew to appreciate being woken up, its been a guest favorite at the Smokehouse.

MAKES 1 SANDWICH

INGREDIENTS

1 sandwich bun

5 ounces beef brisket

4 tablespoons All-Purpose BBQ Sauce (page 25)

2 fried onion rings, from your favorite recipe

4 to 6 jalapeño slices

1 slice provolone cheese

METHOD

Preheat oven to 375°F.

On bottom half of sandwich bun, layer brisket followed by sauce, onion rings, jalapeños, and cheese.

Bake open-faced for 5 minutes or until cheese is melted.

Cover with top half of bun, cut in half, and serve hot.

COCHON DE LAIT SANDWICH

MEANING "PIG IN MILK," this Cajun classic came to us by way of Jeff's affinity for New Orleans and a local sandwich served at one of the food booths during Jazz Fest. Folks are known to wait up in line to make sure they get one of the legendary specialties before the "Cochon Lady" sells out, which she always does. One of the keys to this sandwich is using a freshly baked baguette that's crunchy on the outside and light and fluffy on the inside. **MAKES 1 SANDWICH**

COCHON PORK

1 cup coarse salt

1 cup sugar

¾ cup black pepper

¼ cup granulated garlic

2 tablespoons cayenne pepper

1 (7-pound) pork butt

FOR ASSEMBLY

6-inch-long piece of French bread

2 to 3 tablespoons creole mustard

2 tablespoons cabbage, thinly shredded

5 ounces pulled cochon pork

2 dashes hot sauce

MAKE PORK

Soak hickory wood in water for 1 hour and preheat smoker to 225°F.

Combine salt, sugar, black pepper, garlic, and cayenne in a small bowl to make a rub. Season pork liberally with about 1¼ cups of the rub.

Place pork on smoker and smoke for 12 to 16 hours or until internal temperature reaches 190°F. Add more wood and charcoal periodically to maintain a constant temperature.

Remove pork from smoker, wrap tightly in clear plastic wrap, and let rest in a cooler or under a towel for 1 hour before pulling.

Pull pork apart in bite-size pieces.

ASSEMBLE

Cut bread lengthwise, almost, but not quite, in half.

Spread each side with Creole mustard.

Layer with cabbage and pork, then top with hot sauce.

TIP

Since *cochon de lait* means "pig in milk," before cooking you can soak the pork butt overnight in buttermilk with a tablespoon of the cochon pork rub to produce an even more succulent smoked butt.

Jeff and Meredith at Jazz Fest

PHONEY BALONEY

GROWING UP IN a modest household, our school lunches were often bologna and mayonnaise on white bread. To give this protein wonder the honor it deserved, I was determined to come up with a sandwich worthy of the esteemed dietary heritage that bologna held in my youth. Start off by asking your butcher for 1-inch-thick rounds of bologna. Most supermarkets have whole rounds (or tubes) of bologna in the deli case. At the restaurant, we smoke the bologna first, then grill it to combine the charred and smoky flavors, but you can skip the smoking step and the sandwich will be just as delicious. **MAKES 1 SANDWICH**

SANDWICH

1 teaspoon oil

1 4-ounce slice bologna (1-inch-thick cut round)

2 tablespoons 4R Mustard Relish (recipe follows)

Sandwich bun

1 to 2 fried onion rings, from your favorite recipe

1 slice provolone cheese

2 to 3 tablespoons Southern Coleslaw (page 57)

All-Purpose BBQ Sauce (page 25)

MUSTARD RELISH

½ cup yellow mustard (French's or similar)

¼ cup jalapenos, chopped, seeds and veins removed

⅓ cup dill pickles, chopped

MAKE RELISH

Combine all ingredients. Let chill before serving.

MAKE SANDWICH

Preheat oven to 375°F. Heat grill to medium-high.

Brush one side of bologna round with oil and grill for 2 minutes, oiled side down; turn 90 degrees and continue to grill for another 2 minutes, until char lines are dark.

Brush top side of bologna with oil, flip, and repeat grilling procedure until well charred.

Spread relish on top and bottom of bun. Layer grilled bologna, onion rings, and cheese on bun.

Place in oven and bake for 5 minutes or until cheese is melted.

Top with coleslaw and BBQ sauce. Serve hot.

BREADED PORKLETTE WITH CHIPOTLE AIOLI

WHEN ASKED BY the James Beard House to create a "JBH-worthy" dish to support its scholarship fund, we paid homage to our good friends at Chick-fil-A by recasting their famous chicken sandwich—with pork and a few other twists, of course. The brine drives flavor from within the pork, while the peppery-sweet combination of the arugula and chipotle aioli complement the crunchy panko crust. Don't allow a dislike of pickles to keep you from using them. The cool and salty crunch is key to balancing the multiple flavors in this sandwich. **MAKES 6 SANDWICHES**

FRIED PORK CUTLETS

6 (5- to 6-ounce) boneless pork loin cutlets

4 cups buttermilk

3 teaspoons All-Purpose Rub (page 25)

3 teaspoons hot sauce (such as Texas Pete)

3 garlic cloves, smashed

3 cups panko (Japanese bread crumbs)

Vegetable oil

CHIPOTLE AIOLI

½ Granny Smith apple

¾ cup mayonnaise

1½ tablespoons chipotle peppers, pureed

2 tablespoons whole-grain mustard

2 tablespoons apple butter

½ tablespoon Worcestershire sauce

½ tablespoon cider vinegar

½ teaspoon freshly ground black pepper

½ teaspoon granulated garlic

½ teaspoon coarse salt

ARUGULA DRESSING

¼ cup plus 2 tablespoons cider vinegar

½ cup light olive oil

½ cup extra-virgin olive oil

SANDWICHES

3 cups baby arugula

¼ cup plus 2 tablespoons arugula dressing

12 tablespoons chipotle aioli, divided

6 buns

6 fried pork cutlets

12 dill pickle chips

MARINATE PORK CUTLETS

Place each cutlet between 2 pieces of plastic wrap and lightly pound with a meat mallet to shape roughly to the size of a burger bun. Do not pound hard enough to break wrap or penetrate cutlet completely.

Combine buttermilk, rub, hot sauce, and garlic in a large, shallow dish or large zip-top bag. Add pork cutlets, turning to coat in marinade. Cover tightly and marinate 2 days.

MAKE AIOLI

Preheat oven to 350°F. Peel apple and cut into thin slices. Place on a sheet pan and roast for 15 to 20 minutes. Remove from oven, cool, and finely chop.

Stir together 2 tablespoons chopped roasted apple and remaining ingredients in a bowl. Refrigerate until ready to use.

MAKE ARUGULA DRESSING

Whisk together all ingredients in a medium bowl. Use immediately.

MAKE SANDWICHES

Remove cutlets from marinade, shaking off excess. Spread panko on a large plate. Press each cutlet in panko, forming a crust.

Preheat a large pot filled with 3 inches vegetable oil over medium heat. When oil reaches 325°F, fry pork cutlets, a few at a time, until golden brown, 2 to 3 minutes on each side.

Drain on a plate lined with paper towels.

Toss arugula with dressing just before assembling.

Spread top and bottom of each bun with 2 tablespoons aioli (1 tablespoon on each half). Place 2 pickle chips on the bottom of each bun. Top with a fried pork cutlet and ½ cup dressed arugula. Serve immediately.

BEEF

SMOKED BRISKET

GROWING UP IN FLORIDA, BBQ meant pork and chicken. Sausage was unheard of, and the "beef" offered by a few brave barbecue joints was nothing more than chopped, overcooked, dry rump cuts.

Folks from Texas, Oklahoma, and Kansas City have been perfecting smoked brisket for generations. Some contend that the tycoons of the 1800s gave the cheaper cut of beef to their laborers on ranches because the public wouldn't buy it. Over time, the laborers learned to cook the brisket at low temperatures over long periods to break down the fibers and ultimately turn the otherwise leathery meat into a tender piece of beef. Others suggest that Germans immigrated to Texas around the same time and opened a vast array of Bavarian-style butcher shops that used smoking as an effective way to cure and preserve the excess meat for future consumption.

While its origin may be a mystery, the recipe for a successful smoked brisket is not. It took me 18 years of painful and misguided attempts, but I ultimately concluded that there are four simple keys to a succulent brisket:

1. BEEF: Brisket is made up of two separate muscles completely opposite in nature (one lean, the other fatty) held together by connective tissue. The thinner, lean side is called the "point," and the thicker, fattier side is called the "flat" or "deckle." Both are covered with a thick layer of fat called the "fat cap."

For best results, use a whole brisket (both muscles, the point, and the flat) and smoke it with the full fat-cap intact and untrimmed. The fat cap will act as a natural source of moisture, basting the meat and helping to prevent drying. The worst thing you can do is smoke a trimmed point. Trust me when I say that it will more closely resemble a hockey puck than a piece of beef after 12 hours in the smoker.

As with any cut of beef, you get what you pay for. Though I don't think it's necessary to pay for a prime grade of beef, buying a choice grade or above makes a difference in both taste and tenderness. Aging the brisket from 27 to 32 days makes a tremendous difference in the taste, since it naturally extracts the excess water from the beef, producing a more pronounced beef flavor.

2. RUB: Use the same spices that you would put on a steak: kosher salt, a larger grind of black pepper, and perhaps a touch of granulated garlic or onion powder. During the extended cooking period, the rub hardens to create a crisp outside (the bark), while locking in the juices and rich beef flavor. Don't be shy when you're applying the rub—remember there's a lot of meat under the crust that will need to share the flavors of the rub.

3. WOOD: The type of wood used for smoking varies by region and is influenced greatly by availability. Mesquite is best known for Texas barbecue, but use it sparingly or it can become overpowering. Oak is a safe choice for larger cuts that require longer cooking times, since it burns slowly and produces a mild flavor. My preference is hickory. The sweet flavor of hickory complements most meat nicely and the element of smoke is distinct yet not overpowering.

Whatever wood you choose, be sure it is fresh (or green), since wood loses its flavor as it ages. Old wood can produce soot that will cover your meat with a black film.

4. TEMPERATURE: Effectively monitoring and controlling two temperatures is key to a succulent brisket: the temperature inside the smoker and the internal temperature of the brisket itself.

Smoking is similar to the curing process, requiring a consistency in the environment over an extended period of time. With brisket, the old saying of "lid it and forget it" couldn't ring more true. Maintaining a consistent temperature between 215° to 225°F is essential in creating the balance between the hard, outside crust and the moist, tender inside. Fluctuations or spikes in temperature will result in the meat cooking too fast, which will dry it out and not allow the bark to form properly, thus compromising the tenderness. The importance of establishing a thick bark is to retain the moisture.

The USDA recommends an internal temperature for beef of 160°F for medium and 170°F for well-done. However, it's necessary for brisket to reach an internal temp of 190°F in order to break down the collagen fibers that bind the muscle and make it tough. Keeping the full fat cap on to baste the meat over the longer cooking period is key in reaching the higher internal temperature without drying out the brisket. No matter how tempted you are to increase the temperature in hopes of decreasing the cooking time ... don't do it. You'll only end up compromising the end result of your hard work.

Though recognizably the hardest of four keys to master, nothing will have as much impact on your brisket as the proper control and monitoring of the internal and external temperatures. Don't be discouraged by your first attempts. Smoking a good brisket is well worth the time and effort. And I'm willing to bet that, unlike me, it won't take you 18 years. **SERVES 20 OR MORE**

BRISKET

1 whole brisket, 10 to 15 pounds, untrimmed with full fat cap

1 cup All-Purpose Brisket Rub (page 25)

All-Purpose BBQ Sauce (page 25)

Sliced dill pickles

Onions, sliced thin

White bread

PREPARE BRISKET

Apply rub liberally on brisket, making sure to cover all sides and crevices. Refrigerate uncovered at least 4 hours, preferably overnight.

Remove brisket from refrigerator at least 1 hour before smoking, letting it cool to room temperature.

PREPARE SMOKER

Soak hickory chips or chunks for 1 hour before smoking. Soaking will allow the wood to smolder and smoke for longer periods of time versus catching on fire and quickly burning up.

Light charcoal and allow to burn to a white ash.

Place soaked wood on top of hot coals and adjust smoker vents to settle the temperature in a range between 215°F and 225°F.

SMOKE BRISKET

Place brisket, fat side up, indirectly over the smoking wood. Close the lid and get comfortable. Depending on the size of your brisket, smoking will take from 12 to 18 hours. A general rule of thumb is 75 minutes for every pound of brisket.

Keep an eye on your coals and wood, replenishing both as needed, but opening the lid of the smoker as little as possible.

After 8 to 10 hours, check the internal temperature of brisket using a meat thermometer inserted into brisket at its thickest point. Continue checking every 30 to 60 minutes until the internal temperature reaches 190°F to 192°F.

Remove brisket from smoker. Using multiple layers to prevent dripping, wrap brisket in plastic wrap and place in a small, empty cooler. Cover with a folded towel (or two), close the cooler lid, and let it rest for 1 to 2 hours before carving. This will allow the juices to settle back into the meat.

SLICE BRISKET

When ready to serve, remove brisket from cooler and place in a baking sheet or sheet pan with a rim. Carefully cut open the plastic wrap, allowing the juices to spill out into the pan.

Place the whole brisket on a cutting board and, starting at the thinnest part of the flat end, begin to slice

PHOTO BY MICHAEL PISARRI

the brisket against the grain, working toward the thicker side (the point). Trim the fat cap off as necessary, or to your preference.

As you work your way up the brisket, you'll begin to notice a seam of fat forming in the middle of the brisket. This is the connective tissue that holds the two pieces of meat together. Once it becomes distinct and runs the entire width of the brisket, you need to separate the two cuts.

Using a long knife and cutting the full width of the brisket, slice directly into seam of fat, along the contours of the meat, until the two pieces are separated.

Remove the point, flip it over, and, using the back of your knife, scrape the excess fat from the meat. Repeat on the bottom piece.

Rotate the point 90 degrees so the grains of both pieces are running in the same direction. Flip both pieces over so the bark is facing up and continue carving as needed.

Serve with white bread, pickles, onions, and sauce.

CHICKEN-FRIED STEAK

DESPITE THE POPULAR misconception, chicken-fried steak is a beef dish and should be cooked like steak, preferably to about medium doneness to preserve moisture, as opposed to fried chicken, where a little pink sends folks running. Resist the temptation to double-dip in the flour and milk. A single dip allows the crust to get crunchy without masking the flavor of the steak. Down-home faithful believe gravy is the perfect topping that pulls all of the flavors together. And I agree. **SERVES 4 TO 6**

CHICKEN FLOUR

1 cup all-purpose flour

1 tablespoon coarse salt

1 tablespoon coarsely ground black pepper

¼ teaspoon granulated garlic

¼ teaspoon onion powder

CHICKEN FRIED STEAK

2 pounds cube steak

Coarse salt, to taste

Freshly ground black pepper, to taste

1½ cups milk

2 eggs

Vegetable oil, for frying

GRAVY

¼ cup hot bacon grease

⅓ cup flour

2 cups milk

Freshly ground black pepper, to taste

Coarse salt, to taste

MAKE CHICKEN FLOUR

Mix all ingredients in a pie pan or flat baking dish.

PREPARE STEAK

Sprinkle steak with salt and pepper and place between two pieces of plastic wrap.

Pound softly with a meat mallet (spiked side), being careful not to break the wrap.

Set aside, covered, and allow steak to reach room temperature (about 30 minutes).

MAKE CHICKEN FRIED STEAK

Preheat oven to 250°F.

Whisk together milk and eggs in a pie pan or baking dish.

Remove meat from wrap and place in milk mixture, covering completely with milk.

Remove from milk, allowing excess to drip off, then dredge on both sides in chicken flour.

Pour enough oil in a heavy skillet to cover the bottom. Heat to 350°F over medium-high heat, or until oil thins and begins to ripple.

Add meat in batches, being careful not to overcrowd pan. Cook until golden brown, about 4 minutes on each side.

Remove meat from oil and place on a cookie cooling

rack set on a baking sheet. Place rack and sheet in oven to keep warm.

MAKE GRAVY

Heat bacon grease in a skillet over medium-high heat.

Sprinkle flour evenly into bacon grease, whisking continuously until roux turns a light golden brown. Season with pepper while whisking.

Whisk in milk and bring to a boil. Add salt and additional pepper, reduce heat, and simmer until gravy thickens, 5 to 10 minutes. Serve over steaks.

TIP

The gravy needs a good amount of seasonings to produce flavor. The bacon grease will provide a fair amount of salt, but you'll need to be generous with the pepper. You'll know you have enough when black specks are clearly visible throughout your gravy.

SANTA MARIA TRI-TIP

THIS DISH HAS its origins outside of the South and is still somewhat of a regional California specialty, but it is so flavorful that it deserves wider popularity. Tri-tip, as the name implies, is a triangular cut of beef from the bottom sirloin that is the mainstay of barbecues along California's Central Coast. We developed this recipe when we were invited to cater a party in Hollywood for a bunch of actor-type friends. We kept true to the regional flavors, but changed the chimichurri sauce to give it a little oomph. **SERVES 6**

4R SMOKY TOMATO CHIMICHURRI SAUCE
Makes about 3½ cups

2 tablespoons Champagne vinegar

4 tablespoons fresh lemon juice

2 tablespoons garlic, finely minced

1½ teaspoons sea salt

¾ teaspoon dried oregano

½ teaspoon red pepper flakes

¾ teaspoon paprika

1¼ cups extra-virgin olive oil

⅓ cup Smoked Tomatoes, diced (refer to first step for Smoked Tomato Jam, page 48)

1½ cups chopped fresh parsley

½ cup chopped cilantro

SANTA MARIA TRI-TIP

1 (3- to 4-pound) tri-tip roast

2 tablespoons Coffee Rub (page 131)

¾ cup brisket renderings or olive oil

2 tablespoons soy sauce

¼ cup Worcestershire sauce

⅓ cup brown sugar

¼ teaspoon granulated garlic

½ teaspoon coarsely ground black pepper

MAKE CHIMICHURRI SAUCE

Mix together vinegar, lemon juice, garlic, salt, oregano, pepper flakes, and paprika in a mixing bowl. Whisk in olive oil. Gently fold in tomatoes. Refrigerate until ready to serve. Just before serving, stir in parsley and cilantro.

MAKE TRI-TIP

Preheat smoker to 220°F. Season meat lightly with Coffee Rub.

Smoke meat at 220°F for 20 to 30 minutes, or until internal temperature reaches 100°F.

Stir together brisket renderings or olive oil, soy sauce, Worcestershire sauce, brown sugar, garlic, and pepper in a bowl.

Remove brisket from smoker; marinate in mixture for 30 to 45 minutes. Meanwhile, preheat a well-oiled grill to medium-high.

Remove meat from marinade and place on hot grill, rolling until all sides are crusted and caramelized. Internal temperature should be 115°F to 120°F. Remove from grill, loosely tent in foil, and allow to rest 10 minutes before slicing.

Slice across the grain in thin pieces, drizzling juices back onto meat. Top with chimichurri sauce. Serve immediately.

BACON- AND SPINACH-STUFFED RIBEYE ROAST

(Inspired by Bruce Aidells)

I SAW A PICTURE of this in *Bon Appétit* and immediately thought, "Christmas dinner main dish!" Bold yet elegant, this surprisingly easy recipe is sure to impress when brought to the table. Really, what's not to like about it? Big, bone-in ribeyes presented in a half crown with a savory Parmesan-spinach stuffing. Have that special bottle of your biggest, boldest red ready to go because you're sure to need it once the carving begins. **SERVES 6–8**

RIBEYE ROAST

15-bone standing ribeye roast (about 10-14 pounds), chine bone removed and fat trimmed to ¼ inch thick

2 tablespoons olive oil

Coarse salt

Freshly ground black pepper

¼ cup fresh thyme, minced

BACON AND SPINACH STUFFING

8 ounces hickory or applewood smoked bacon, chopped

¾ cup yellow onion, minced

¾ cup celery, minced

2 garlic cloves, minced

1 tablespoon fresh rosemary, minced

1 tablespoon fresh thyme, minced

1 tablespoon coarse salt

2 tablespoons freshly ground black pepper

2 cups cooked spinach, squeezed dry, chopped

¼ cup pine nuts, toasted

1½ cups Panko bread crumbs

1 extra large egg, whisked

6 tablespoons butter, melted

½ cup fresh Parmesan, grated

¼ cup flat-leaf parsley, chopped

½ cup beef broth

MAKE STUFFING

Sauté bacon until crisp in a large skillet over medium heat. Add onion, celery, garlic, rosemary, thyme, salt, and pepper; cook until onions are translucent. Stir in spinach and cook for 5 minutes. Remove from heat and cool slightly.

Place pine nuts in a food processor and pulse 3-4 times until rough chopped. Combine nuts with bread crumbs, egg, butter, cheese, and parsley in large mixing bowl. Stir in spinach mixture.

Add beef broth gradually and mix well, making sure stuffing is firm to touch. Set aside.

TIP

Ask your butcher to remove the chine bone and trim the fat to an even ¼-inch thickness, and you'll save a good amount of time and guess work.

COOK ROAST

Let meat stand at room temperature for 3 hours before cooking.

Preheat oven to 425°F. Arrange racks so roast will be on bottom third of oven.

Place roast on work surface, standing bones straight up. Wrap 3 "extended" rib bones with foil to prevent burning. Cut along bones with sharp knife, leaving only 1 inch of meat attached at base of bones, being careful not to cut all the way through roast.

Season entire roast with olive oil, salt, and pepper; sprinkle with thyme. "Open" roast and continue seasoning inside of meat. Place stuffing on bone side, making sure to cover completely and pack firmly. Close roast back up. If any stuffing remains, place in prepared dish and bake during the last 20 minutes of roast cooking.

Tie twine horizontally around roast to keep stuffing in place. Tie roast vertically between each bone. Cover ends of roast with foil to keep stuffing in place. Set prepared V-shaped rack into large roasting pan. Place roast on rack.

Roast for 20 minutes, then reduce heat to 350°F and continue roasting for another 2 hours, checking the thermometer until it reaches preferred doneness—110°F to 115°F for medium-rare. (Meat will continue to cook once removed from oven.)

Place roast on carving board, and let rest for 30 minutes before slicing. Serve immediately.

OXTAIL BEEF STEW

ONCE CONSIDERED EXCLUSIVE to soul food, oxtail has risen to an esteemed position in Southern cooking primarily due to the rich beef flavor resulting from the generous amount of marrow released while cooking. You can certainly use other cuts of beef if you can't find oxtail. I often add chuck-eye roast or beef short ribs to help fill the pot and add a little diversity.

The key to a rich yet moist stew is in the proper searing of the beef on the front end. When searing, use generous amounts of seasonings, and don't overcrowd the pan. Doing so will release too much moisture and will end up steaming the meat versus browning it.

And, for all those with queasy tummies, oxtail comes from a regular ol' cow and has nothing to do with an actual ox. **SERVES 6**

INGREDIENTS

4 pounds oxtails, cut into 1-inch-thick shanks (can add chuck-eye roast or beef short ribs)

Vegetable oil

Coarse salt

Freshly ground black pepper

8 slices bacon

4 tablespoons unsalted butter, divided, room temperature

1 cup hearty red wine such as Syrah or Zinfandel

1 large sweet onion, chopped

3 large carrots, peeled and cut into 1- to 2-inch chunks

3 celery stalks, cut into ½-inch lengths

2 garlic cloves, chopped

6 tablespoons all-purpose flour

4 cups beef stock

2 tablespoons tomato paste

1 tablespoon flat-leaf parsley, chopped

1 teaspoon fresh thyme, chopped

1 teaspoon fresh rosemary, chopped

1 bay leaf

2 pounds red-skinned potatoes, unpeeled and cut into 1-inch cubes

METHOD

Preheat oven to 325°F.

Lightly coat oxtail shanks with oil, then generously add salt and pepper. Cover, set aside, and allow to reach room temperature.

In large Dutch oven, cook bacon until crisp. Reserving grease in the pot, remove bacon, chop, and keep it for later.

Bring heat to medium-high. Add oxtail in batches to avoid overcrowding. Resist the urge to touch it. Allow to sear about 4 to 5 minutes until it sticks to the pan. Flip and sear other side, another 5 minutes or so. Remove from pot, repeat with remaining pieces. Add additional oil as needed.

Keep heat at medium-high and add wine. Using a wooden spoon, scrape bits and pieces of meat from bottom of pan. When wine is reduced by half, lower heat to medium and add 2 tablespoons of butter, onion, carrot, celery, and garlic. Cook, stirring occasionally until onion softens, about 5 minutes. Add pinch of salt and pepper. Reduce heat to low.

In a bowl, combine flour and remaining 2 tablespoons of butter to make a paste. Using a wooden spoon, gradually add stock to paste while stirring to blend. Continue to do so until paste is thinned, then add to pot, stirring constantly until well incorporated. Increase heat to medium; simmer and let thicken, about 15 minutes, stirring occasionally.

Add tomato paste, parsley, thyme, rosemary, and bay leaf. Mix well to blend.

Return oxtail and chopped bacon to pot and bring to boil. Remove from stove, cover, place in oven, and cook for 1½ hours.

Remove from oven. Add potatoes and a pinch of salt and pepper. Stir to blend. Cover and return to oven for another 45 minutes, until potatoes are cooked. Remove from oven.

Skim top of sauce with a spoon to capture and remove the layer of floating fat.

Season with salt and pepper to taste, and serve with crusty bread and remaining wine.

Recipe can be made a day ahead. Allow to cool, cover, and refrigerate. To serve, reheat in 300°F oven, covered, stirring occasionally, until warm.

COFFEE-CRUSTED COWBOY RIBEYE STEAK

IF YOU WANT to grill a steak the way they did it in the Old West, nothing beats a thick "Cowboy" cut bone-in ribeye. A Cowboy steak is a 2- to 3-inch-thick ribeye with the bone attached, usually weighing in at about 2 pounds and generously marbled, making it both visually impressive and incredibly juicy and tender.

Cowboys used the protruding bone as a handle to hold the steak over the flames of an open campfire. For home cooking, grilling over charcoal (or gas, if forced) is the best approach to get the great woody flavor and the desired charred crust. The heat generated from the briquettes is typically greater than what you get from a home stovetop range and necessary to produce the dark, charred outer crust that encases the pink, tender inside where the moisture retreats from the intense heat.

When grilling over an open flame, a thicker cut is your best bet for protection against the flare-ups that happen when grease drips on the coals. These flare-ups are necessary to produce the charred outer coat that acts as a barrier to retain the beef's moisture. Plus, the texture and taste of charred meat adds a balance to the velvety, moisture-rich inside.

The key to achieving this nirvana state of beef balance is to resist the urge to flip the steak more than once while grilling. Leave it alone. Let it sit and allow the flames to do their job. The more intense the heat, the faster the outside will sear and the inside juices will be trapped. Flipping only releases juice and slows the crusting process, thus pushing the seared area farther into the protected middle. **SERVES 2**

COWBOY RIB-EYE STEAK

1 (16- to 18-ounce) ribeye steak, bone in, 2 to 3 inches thick. (Ask your butcher for a French cut if you want to show off a bit.)

4 tablespoons Coffee Rub (recipe follows), or a 50-50 blend of kosher salt and coarse pepper

1 medium onion, thinly sliced

3 garlic cloves, finely minced

1 cup (2 sticks) unsalted butter, softened, divided

COFFEE RUB
Makes 2½ cups

1 cup kosher salt

1 cup coarsely black pepper

¼ cup brown sugar

2 tablespoons ground coffee

2 teaspoons paprika

1 teaspoon cayenne pepper

1 teaspoon dried oregano

1 teaspoon onion powder

1 teaspoon granulated garlic

CONTINUED

MAKE COFFEE RUB

Combine all ingredients until well blended. Store in a dry cool place for up to 30 days.

MAKE STEAK

Rub steak on both sides with coffee rub at least 1 hour (up to 24 hours) before serving. Wrap tightly in plastic wrap and refrigerate. Remove 1 hour before grilling and let come to room temperature.

Preheat oven to 325°F and preheat grill to high.

Sauté onion and garlic in ½ cup butter in a large sauté pan (big enough to hold the steak) over medium heat until onion is translucent, about 5 minutes. Remove pan from heat and set aside.

Place steak on grill directly over the hottest area and sear for 4 minutes without moving. Flip once and repeat.

Remove steak from grill and place in sauté pan with garlic and onions, covering steak with onions.

Divide remaining ½ cup butter into small pats and put on steak. Finish steak in oven for 4 to 7 minutes for medium-rare and 7 to 10 minutes for medium, turning once and spooning melted butter over the top of the steak.

Remove pan from oven. Remove steak from sauté pan, tent with foil, and let rest for 10 minutes before slicing.

Serve with melted butter and onions.

TIP

Ultra-thick, Flintstone-size, bone-in steaks require a bit of extra care when cooking. Their thick size makes them all too easy to end up with a burnt exterior and cold, raw middle. To protect against this, increase the baking time versus the grilling time. Doing so allows the inside a chance to catch up with the charred outer crust.

BRISKET AND CHEESE GRITS SHEPHERD'S PIE

EACH SATURDAY, when I'm not traveling, I try to create a brand-new dish. I spend the week pouring through cookbooks, foraging for ideas, so come Saturday I can go to work creating a new dish. It's great fun for me and tends to result in some pretty interesting family-style meals for the team.

This was one of my Saturday creations. Shepherd's pie is a staple in the world of comfort food, and replacing the traditional ground beef with smoked brisket adds even more comfort. Combining the cheese grits with the potatoes places this dish square in the Southern Cowboy crosshairs. **SERVES 8**

PIE FILLING

4 slices bacon, chopped

4 tablespoons butter (½ stick), room temperature

1 cup onion, diced

½ cup carrots, diced

2 cloves garlic, minced

¼ teaspoon ground thyme

1 tablespoon fresh rosemary, chopped

1 tablespoon salt

2 tablespoons pepper

½ pound smoked brisket (can substitute ribeye or short rib), finely chopped

2 tablespoons Worcestershire sauce

2 Smoked Tomatoes (refer to first step for Smoked Tomato Jam, page 48), or ½ cup canned stewed tomatoes

1½ cups beef stock

2 tablespoons flour

1 cup Smokehouse Corn (page 63), or frozen corn, thawed

1 cup Southern Green Beans (page 194), or frozen green beans, thawed

TOPPING

2½ pounds potatoes

6 cups chicken stock

½ cup half-and-half

3 tablespoons butter

1 tablespoon salt

1 tablespoon pepper

¼ cup whipped cream cheese

1 cup Cheese Grits

½ cup cheddar cheese, shredded

CHEESE GRITS

½ teaspoon freshly ground black pepper

2 tablespoons unsalted butter

3 cups of chicken stock

1 cup heavy cream

½ teaspoon hot sauce, such as Pete's or Tabasco

½ teaspoon salt

¼ teaspoon granulated garlic

1⅛ cups old-fashioned grits (not instant!)

8 ounces extra-sharp cheddar cheese (about 2 cups), grated

MAKE FILLING

Over medium-high heat, fry bacon to a crisp in a large pan. Remove from pan, reserving the grease in the pan, and set aside for later use.

Add 2 tablespoons of butter to pan and sauté onion on medium-high for 3 minutes. Add carrots, garlic, rosemary, thyme, salt and pepper, and continue to sauté until onions are translucent, about 5 minutes.

Add chopped meat, tomatoes, Worcestershire sauce, and beef stock and bring to a boil. Reduce heat to medium and sauté for 20 minutes, stirring occasionally.

In a separate bowl, combine remaining 2 tablespoon of butter and flour.

Mix until a paste is formed. Add 2 tablespoons of the filling sauce to the paste, whisking to incorporate. Repeat 3 times or until paste is thinned, then add to the filling sauce simmering in the pan.

Add green beans and corn and continue to sauté for another 10 minutes. Remove from heat, and set aside until ready for assembly. Taste for seasoning. Can be done 1 to 2 days in advance.

MAKE CHEESE GRITS

Cook black pepper and butter in a large saucepan over medium heat until butter is melted. Add chicken stock, cream, hot sauce, and salt; bring to a boil.

CONTINUED

Whisk in the grits and reduce the heat to low. Cook, stirring frequently, until grits are thick and creamy, about 15 minutes.

MAKE TOPPING

Pour chicken stock into a pot, cover with lid tightly, and bring to a boil. Add potatoes, cover, and reduce heat to medium-high for 20 to 25 minutes or until potatoes are fork tender. Remove from heat.

Using care, transfer potatoes to a colander and rinse under cold water for 1 to 2 minutes until no longer hot.

Set potato ricer over the warm pot. Working in batches, place potatoes into ricer hopper and press, removing any potatoes stuck to bottom. If a ricer isn't available, a potato masher or a large whisk will work.

Add all of the ingredients except for the half-and-half to the potatoes. Using a rubber spatula, stir until incorporated. Stir in warm half-and-half until incorporated. Season to taste with additional salt and pepper, if needed. Use immediately while hot.

ASSEMBLE AND BAKE PIE

If using a cold filling, warm in a pan over medium heat for 20 minutes, stirring occasionally to bring back to temperature.

Preheat oven to 400°F.

Spoon warm pie filling into a 9-by-12-inch casserole dish or two 9-inch pie pans. Fill to about 75 percent and top with mashed potatoes. Spread the potatoes evenly across the top of the filling until they're flush against the inner walls and reach the top of the dish.

Place pie atop a cooking sheet, and bake for 25 minutes or until peaks of potatoes are browned. Remove from oven and rest on a cooling rack for 15 minutes before serving.

STREET TACOS

FEW THINGS BETTER reflect the heart and soul of a city than the food you find in the humblest of joints or on the corners of the busiest streets. When in Mexico, I lose all semblance of tasting caution and restraint. The sound of meat sizzling over hot coals combined with the bold aroma of the peppers, onions, and cilantro emanating from these little makeshift kitchens sends me into a tasting frenzy. Though my enthusiasm has certainly gotten the best of me by the following morning, it's yet to deter my determination to go back for more ... again and again.

I wanted to create the same explosion of flavors I found on the street but with a Smokehouse twist. We did so by introducing smoked brisket and pork to the otherwise true-to-form street-taco staples of fresh pico de gallo, warm corn tortillas, and crumbled queso blanco. You can take your choice of the sauces, but I like to load up with all of them. The only thing missing is a shot of tequila. **MAKES 12 TACOS**

12 (4-inch) corn tortillas

1½ pounds smoked beef brisket, chicken, or pork, shredded

½ cup queso blanco, crumbled

Fresh jalapeños and cilantro for garnish, chopped

Habanero Sauce

Guasacaca Sauce

Pico de Gallo (page 33)

Cilantro Crème Fraîche (page 33)

GUASACACA SAUCE

1 large onion, roughly chopped

2 green peppers, seeded, deveined, and roughly chopped

2 avocados, peeled and seeded

1 tablespoon garlic, minced

½ bunch flat-leaf parsley leaves, roughly chopped

½ bunch cilantro leaves, roughly chopped

⅓ cup red wine vinegar

1½ tablespoons salt

¼ teaspoon black pepper

1 jalapeño, seeded, deveined, and chopped

1 cup olive oil

HABANERO SAUCE

1½ pounds red habanero peppers, seeded, deveined, and roughly chopped

2 large onions, roughly chopped

2 green peppers, roughly chopped

1¾ cups white vinegar

2 teaspoons kosher salt

2 tablespoons olive oil

TIP

The pico de gallo is best if allowed to sit covered and refrigerated for a couple of hours before serving.

MAKE GUASACACA SAUCE

Put all ingredients except olive oil into a food processor and blend until smooth, working in batches if necessary. Add olive oil in a stream with processor running and combine until smooth. Let stand at room temperature for at least 1 hour.

MAKE HABANERO SAUCE

Preheat oven to 300°F. Coat peppers and onions in olive oil, spread on sheet tray, and roast until soft, 20 to 30 minutes. In a blender or food processor, puree vegetables, adding vinegar and salt. Set aside until ready to use.

MAKE TACOS

Heat tortillas in a dry skillet or on the grill, 30 seconds each side.

Evenly divide shredded meat in each tortilla.

Top with pico de gallo, queso blanco, Guasacaca Sauce, Habanero Sauce, and dollop of crème fraîche.

Garnish with chopped jalapeños and cilantro.

PHOTO BY MELISSA SPILMAN

OSSO BUCCO

I APPRECIATE THAT this is a fancy dish for a cowboy, but it's one of my very favorites and, when cooked properly, deserves an honored place at the table. Milanease for "bone with hole," Osso Bucco owes it richness to the marrow in the crosscut veal shank, which oozes out while cooking, adding a meaty, buttery richness to the dish. The recipe benefits from the addition of citrus rinds, which provide a fresh uplift in flavor that complements the hearty, bold flavors of the beef, tomatoes, and wine stock. Like a tomato-based sauce, Osso Buco is best served over pasta, polenta or, my personal preference, Parmesan mashed potatoes. **SERVES 4**

OSSO BUCCO

5 veal shanks, about 1 pound each, trimmed

¼ cup olive oil, divided

1 tablespoon kosher salt

1 tablespoon ground black pepper

2 tablespoons all-purpose flour

Anchovy oil, drained from 2-ounce can

4 tablespoons (½ stick) butter

1 large onion, coarsely chopped

1 large carrot, peeled and cut into 1-inch pieces

2 celery ribs, cut into 1-inch pieces

1 tablespoon fresh thyme, chopped, or 1 teaspoon, dried

2 garlic cloves, mashed

4 anchovy filets, minced

2 cups white wine (a buttery wine such as Conundrum works best)

¼ orange peel, cut into 2 strips

¼ lemon peel, cut into 2 strips

2 cups canned crushed tomatoes, with juice

2 tablespoons flat leaf parsley, chopped

1 tablespoon fresh oregano, chopped, or 1 teaspoon, dried

2 tablespoons fresh basil, chopped, or 2 teaspoons, dried

2 bay leaves

2 cups beef stock

GREMOLATA

¾ cup flat leaf parsley, finely chopped

2 garlic cloves, minced

1 tablespoon orange zest

1 tablespoon fresh basil, finely chopped, or 1 teaspoon, dried

CREME FRAICHE

1 cup whipping cream

2 tablespoons buttermilk

2 tablespoons plain yogurt

FOR SERVING

Prepared pasta, polenta, or mashed potatoes

Grated Parmesan

CONTINUED

MAKE GREMOLATA

Combine all ingredients and mix well. Cover until ready to use.

MAKE CRÈME FRAÎCHE

Combine all ingredients and beat until soft peaks form. Cover and refrigerate until ready to use. Can be made one day ahead.

MAKE OSSO BUCCO

Preheat oven to 275°F.

Rub shanks with olive oil, season with salt and pepper, and dust with flour, shaking off excess.

Heat 2 tablespoons olive oil in deep casserole pot or Dutch oven on medium-high heat. Sear 1 or 2 shanks at a time for 3 to 5 minutes per side until richly browned. Add more oil if needed. Remove shanks and set aside, reserving oil in pot.

Reduce heat to medium. Add anchovy oil, butter, carrots, celery, and onion, and sauté until onions are just turning translucent, about 10 to 15 minutes. Add thyme and garlic, and saute another 5 minutes.

Bring heat to high and add wine. Using wooden spoon, deglaze pot, scraping all pieces from the bottom until wine reduces by half, about 5 minutes. Reduce heat to medium and add crushed tomatoes with juice, anchovies, citrus rinds, crème fraîche, basil, bay leaves, parsley, oregano, and beef broth. Simmer until well incorporated, about 5 minutes. Remove from heat.

Place shanks back in pot if room allows or in deep casserole dish, and pour tomato mixture evenly over shanks until they are 80 percent covered. Reserve remaining mixture.

Cover and roast for 2½ hours, basting every 30 minutes. Uncover and continue roasting for another 30 minutes, until meat is very tender and falling off the bone. Transfer shanks to a large rimmed baking sheet. Cover with foil.

Increase oven temperature to 350°F.

Strain liquid from roasting pan into a saucepan, reserving vegetables. Boil the liquid uncovered until reduced by half, about 30 minutes, stirring occasionally.

Remove sauce from heat and add vegetables. Meanwhile, reheat shanks in oven until hot, about 7 minutes.

ASSEMBLE

Place shanks in rimmed plates over pasta, polenta, or mashed potatoes, and top with sauce and vegetables. Add a sprinkle of gremolata and Parmesan. Enjoy with a crusty bread.

TEQUILA-SPIKED STEAK FAJITAS

ALWAYS GREAT FOR dinner parties, fajitas are as much about "boastful talk" around the grill as they are about the beautiful spread they create alongside the vibrant colors of the accompanying peppers, guacamole, and pico de gallo. Good fajita meat has a crispy-charred outside and a flavorful yet moist and tender inside. The key is to create two adjacent heat zones on your grill: one super-hot, to char, and the other warm, to roast. The marinade will take care of driving the flavor, making it easy to prepare and fun to serve this meal that everyone is sure to enjoy. Accompany with warm tortillas, Mexican yellow rice, and refried beans. **SERVES 6**

TEQUILA-SPIKED STEAK

¾ cup Worcestershire sauce

¼ cup soy sauce

3 tablespoons water

1 tablespoon white vinegar

2 tablespoons fresh lime juice

½ teaspoon garlic powder

½ teaspoon cumin

½ teaspoon dried Mexican oregano

½ teaspoon ground coriander

2 tablespoons good-quality Tequila (optional)

1 tablespoon pineapple juice

¼ teaspoon fresh ginger, grated

¼ cup apple juice

1 tablespoon freshly ground black pepper

½ teaspoon crushed red pepper

⅓ cup cilantro, chopped

2 pounds flank steak

1 large Vidalia onion, cut in half horizontally, first layer of skin removed

2 green peppers, halved, stems and veins removed

2 red peppers, halved, stems and veins removed

1 jalapeño pepper, seeds and veins removed, diced

GUACAMOLE

3 ripe yet firm avocados

1 small onion, diced

1 small tomato, diced

2 tablespoons cilantro, chopped

1 teaspoon fresh lime juice

1 jalapeño pepper, seeds and stems removed, diced

Coarse salt

Freshly ground black pepper, to taste

FAJITAS

12 flour or corn tortillas, 6 or 12 inch

1 whole bunch fresh cilantro, cleaned and tied at stems

2 cups Pico de Gallo (page 33), for serving

½ cup sour cream, for serving

½ cup fresh cilantro, chopped, for serving

1½ cups cheddar, Mexican blend, or Colby/Monterey Jack cheese, shredded, for serving

2 jalapeños, seeds and veins removed, diced, for serving

CONTINUED

PREPARE STEAK

Twenty-four hours before serving, combine first 16 ingredients in a bowl and mix well. Pour in a zip-top bag and add steak, onion, peppers, and cilantro. Seal tight and refrigerate overnight.

MAKE GUACAMOLE

Halve and pit avocados. With a tablespoon, scoop out flesh into a mixing bowl. Mash with a fork, leaving chunky.

Lightly mix in remaining ingredients. Place a piece of plastic wrap directly on top of the guacamole to prevent browning.

Refrigerate at least 1 hour before serving.

MAKE FAJITAS

Remove steak, onion, and peppers from marinade, cover and set aside for 30 minutes to reach room temperature. Reserve marinade in a bowl.

Heat half of grill to high and half to medium heat.

Grill tortillas over medium heat until lightly brown; wrap in foil and set aside to keep warm.

Place reserved marinade next to grill and place the bunch of cilantro in marinade, leaves down.

Place steak on hot side of grill and sear for 2 minutes to char. Use cilantro bunch to brush meat with marinade. Turn and sear other side for 2 minutes, using cilantro to brush with marinade.

Turn steak and move to medium heat for 2 minutes, brushing top with marinade. Turn once more and continue to grill until desired level of doneness, about 2 more minutes for medium.

Transfer steak to a chopping board, tent with foil, and allow to rest for 10 minutes before slicing. Meanwhile, grill vegetables over medium heat, turning once and using cilantro to brush on marinade. Remove from grill and place on chopping board with meat. Discard remaining marinade.

Slice steak against the grain in ½-inch-wide strips. Slice onion and peppers.

Serve with tortillas, guacamole, pico de gallo, and toppings.

Grilling with my son, Jared

BEEF SHORT RIBS WITH RED WINE REDUCTION SAUCE AND COLLARD-INFUSED CHEESE GRITS

WE CAME UP WITH this dish when I was invited to cook at an event alongside Thomas Keller and Daniel Boulud. Given my level of respect for these culinary giants, I knew we had to show up at the dance with more than just our traditional smoked ribs. I love Texas-size smoked beef ribs as much as I do braised short ribs, and this dish gave us the opportunity to combine the two along with another favorite, a hearty Cab. Things came out well, and we were honored for best dish of the night. Not too shabby for a couple of BBQ guys hanging out in the kitchen. **SERVES 4**

BEEF SHORT RIBS

4-pound rack beef short ribs (about 8 ribs), cut into individual ribs

1½ tablespoons Brisket Rub (page 25)

1½ teaspoons granulated garlic

RED WINE REDUCTION SAUCE
Makes 1 cup

1 cup white onion, diced small

2 cloves garlic, minced

2 tablespoons olive oil

1 cup dry red wine (I like a bold Cabernet for this recipe)

1 tablespoon fresh thyme, chopped

1 bay leaf

1½ cups beef stock

2 tablespoons All-Purpose BBQ Sauce (page 25)

1 tablespoon Hot BBQ Sauce (recipe follows)

2 tablespoons brisket demi-glace or favorite store-bought demi-glace

Coarse salt, to taste

Freshly ground black pepper, to taste

1 tablespoon cornstarch

2 tablespoons water

¼ cup parsley, chopped, for garnish

HOT BBQ SAUCE

Use same ingredients as All-Purpose BBQ Sauce (page 25), adding:

1 habanero pepper, seeded, deveined, and chopped

¼ teaspoon cayenne pepper

COLLARD-INFUSED CHEESE GRITS

(page 71)

MAKE SHORT RIBS

Coat ribs with seasoning and garlic.

Place on a hot grill and char on all sides; remove and place in an aluminum pan big enough to hold ribs, and cover loosely with foil.

Place pan in a 250°F smoker; smoke for 2 to 3 hours or until ribs are beginning to pull away from bone.

Remove ribs from pan, reserving juice in pan. Place ribs directly on smoker grate; smoke another 1½ to 2 hours until tender and a dark chocolate color.

Keep reserved juices warm but do not reduce.

Place ribs bone-side up in reserved juices until ready to serve.

MAKE WINE SAUCE

In a saucepan, sauté onion and garlic in olive oil over medium-low heat until onion is translucent, about 5 minutes.

Turn heat to high and deglaze pan with red wine; add thyme and bay leaf.

Bring to a low boil and cook until wine is reduced by half, about 10 minutes. Strain through cheesecloth and keep warm.

Heat beef stock in a saucepan; cook until reduced by half, about 12 to 15 minutes. Stir in BBQ sauces and bring to a simmer. Stir in wine reduction and demi-glace. Taste and add salt and pepper as needed.

In a separate bowl, dissolve cornstarch in lukewarm water, whisking constantly; stir into sauce to thicken.

ASSEMBLE

Spoon a serving of grits onto each plate. Place 2 ribs atop grits, drizzle with wine sauce, and garnish with chopped parsley

PHOTO BY MELISSA SPILMAN

PORK AND LAMB

PULLED PORK

THE HEADLINER IN SOUTHERN BBQ, pulled pork is typically referred to by many from the Deep South simply as "BBQ." Until recently, beef was scarcely found in Southern BBQ restaurants and when it was, it was dried-out sliced rump roast or a failed attempt at brisket that begged pity for the cow that seemingly died in vain.

Perhaps one reason pulled pork is so prevalent is due to the forgiving nature of the cut of pork used, the Boston or pork butt (which is actually from the front shoulders of the pig.) The "butt" benefits greatly from a thick fat cap, as well as an abundance of fat running throughout the cut, and the large center bone called the shoulder blade. When smoked for prolonged periods, the fat acts as a natural moisturizer as it breaks down alongside the seeping marrow from the bone.

The difference between pulled pork and sliced or chopped pork is the ability to easily separate the pork into small strands with a fork or, better yet, your fingers. This happens after the fat fibers and connective tissue between the muscles break down or, more accurately, melt away. This occurs only after the internal temperature of the meat reaches 190°F. USDA standards dictate that whole cuts of meat are done at 145°F (with 3 minutes of resting time.) However, to get the pork to pull apart you'll need to allow the temp to reach 190°F. Hence, the benefit of the fat cap and abundance of fat within the cut.

Generally speaking, I'm not a fan of injecting meats, but it works well with pork butt as it adds flavor to the inside meat where neither the smoke nor the rub are able to reach. When pulled and mixed with the dark flavorful outside crust (called the bark), the combined flavors create a great taste and texture.

I learned this technique from my friend and BBQ circuit icon Chris Lilly of Big Bob Gibson's BBQ in Decatur, Alabama. Long before I had the chance to cook alongside Chris, I would watch his "how-to" BBQ DVD's and practice his techniques in my garage. It truly was an honor to meet Chris the first time cooking at that South Beach Wine & Food Festival back in 2010. Since then we've cooked together at other events and, just like the old days in my garage, I still learn something new from this six-time World Champion BBQ master.

INGREDIENTS

2 bone-in pork butts, about 7 lbs. each, full fat cap on

1 cup Pork Injection (Recipe follows)

1 cup Pulled Pork Mustard Slather (recipe follows)

1 cup All-Purpose Rub (recipe follows)

2 cups of apple juice in a squirt bottle

3 cups Pulled Pork Finishing Sauce (recipe follows)

Chris Lilly and John at the South Beach Wine & Food Festival

PHOTO BY MICHAEL PISARRI

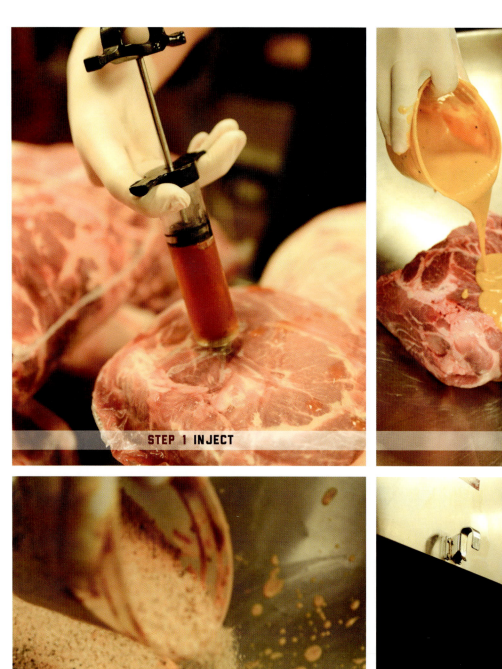
STEP 1 INJECT

STEP 2 SLATHER

STEP 3 RUB

STEP 4 SMOKE AT 225°F

STEP 5 REMOVE AT 192°F INTERNAL TEMPERATURE

STEP 6 ADD FINISHING SAUCE

STEP 7 PULL THE PORK

STEP 8 MAKE SLOPPY AND ENJOY

PULLED PORK INJECTION

MAKES ABOUT 4 CUPS

INGREDIENTS

- 2 cups apple juice or cider
- 1 cup apple cider vinegar
- 1 cup brown sugar
- ¼ cup coarse salt
- 2 tablespoons Worcestershire sauce

METHOD

Mix all ingredients in a large bowl. Cover and refrigerate until ready to use.

PULLED PORK MUSTARD SLATHER

MAKES ABOUT 5¾ CUPS

INGREDIENTS

- 1 can or bottle of beer, allowed to go flat
- 1 cup brown sugar
- 1 teaspoon cumin
- 1 teaspoon freshly ground black pepper
- 1 tablespoon honey
- 4 cups yellow mustard
- 1 teaspoon coarse salt
- 2 teaspoons hot sauce

METHOD

Mix all ingredients in a bowl. Cover and refrigerate until ready to use.

ALL-PURPOSE RUB

MAKES ABOUT ½ CUP

INGREDIENTS

- 2 tablespoons freshly ground black pepper
- 3 tablespoons coarse salt
- 3 tablespoons brown sugar
- 1½ teaspoons garlic powder
- ½ teaspoon chili powder
- ½ teaspoon onion powder
- 1 teaspoon dry mustard
- ½ teaspoon ground red pepper

METHOD

Mix all ingredients in a small bowl. Store in airtight container.

PULLED PORK FINISHING SAUCE

MAKES ABOUT 5 CUPS

INGREDIENTS

4 cups All-Purpose BBQ Sauce (page 25)

4½ cups apple cider vinegar

½ cup brown sugar

1 tablespoon coarse salt

¼ tablespoon freshly ground black pepper

1 cup ketchup

1 tablespoon garlic powder

2 tablespoons crushed red pepper

METHOD

Mix together all ingredients in a bowl. Cover and refrigerate until ready to use.

PREPARE SMOKER

Soak hickory chunks or split logs in water at least 1 hour before smoking.

Light charcoal and allow to burn to a white ash

Place soaked hickory on top of hot coals and allow the smoker temperature to settle at 225°F.

MAKE PORK

Allow pork to sit at room temperature for up to one hour, either covered or in original packaging.

Trim any hard white pockets of fat but don't get carried away with the trimming. You want to keep an even thickness of the fat cap over the top of the butt.

Place pork in a large bowl or on a baking sheet. Use a meat injector to apply the injection sauce into the pork butt about every two inches, with each injection going deep enough to reach the middle of the meat or to the bone.

Cover entirely with mustard slather.

Apply a generous amount of all-purpose rub to meat, making sure the rub gets into any cracks and crevices in the meat. Pat so the rub will stick.

Place in smoker, cover, and smoke over indirect heat for 12 to 16 hours at 225°F or until a meat thermometer stuck in the thickest part of the butt registers 192°F. Check and replace wood and coal every couple of hours to maintain a consistent temperature

After 6 hours, spray the ribs with apple juice every hour. Move quickly when you open the smoker to maintain the temperature.

Pull the pork butt off the smoker when it reaches an internal temp of 192°F. The outside bark should be black and the center bone (blade) will be sticking out from the meat. Tent with foil and allow to cool for 30 minutes.

Using a pair of forks, shred meat into bite-sized pieces, discarding any large pieces of fat. Stir in pulled pork finish. Keep covered tightly until serving to prevent pork from drying.

GRILLED TERIYAKI PORK TENDERLOIN WITH PLUM SAUCE

AN HOMAGE TO my good friend Tom Finn, who puts pineapple on everything, this dish has an Asian twist that pairs the fresh flavors of ginger and pineapple with the sweetness of plum sauce and the savoriness of the pork. The vibrant combination of flavors presents well with grilled veggies over rice. For an extra splash of color and tropical flavor, top it with a slice of grilled pineapple—for my friend Tom. **SERVES 6**

INGREDIENTS

1 cup teriyaki sauce

1 cup plum sauce, divided

1 tablespoon chili garlic sauce

1 tablespoon fresh ginger, peeled and grated

1 cup pineapple juice

3 pounds pork tenderloin

METHOD

Whisk together teriyaki, ½ cup plum sauce, chili garlic sauce, ginger, and pineapple juice in a bowl and pour into a zip-top bag.

Place pork in marinade; seal bag tightly and refrigerate for several hours or overnight.

Remove tenderloin from bag, reserving marinade. Set out for 30 minutes to reach room temperature.

Meanwhile, stir together marinade and remaining plum sauce in a saucepan over medium-high heat. Bring to a boil, then simmer until thick and reduced by half, about 15 minutes.

Light a grill and bring to a medium-high temperature. If using charcoal, push coals to one side of the grill to create a direct and an indirect heating zone.

Place tenderloin directly over hot side of grill and sear for 2 to 3 minutes, until well charred. Flip and sear other side for another 2 to 3 minutes, brushing the top with the reduced marinade.

Reduce the heat to low or slide tenderloin to the indirect side of grill, flip, and brush top with reduced marinade. Close lid of grill and cook, basting and turning every 5 minutes, about 10 to 15 minutes for medium, or until internal temperature reaches 150°F.

Remove meat from grill and loosely cover with foil. Let stand for at least 10 minutes before slicing.

BRAISED LAMB SHANKS

AN ARTICLE IN *Bon Appetit* once stated that braising makes heroes out of weekend kitchen warriors—and I believe it. There are few other cooking techniques that require so little yet return so much. In contrast to the complexity of the succulent flavors in the result, braising involves only four steps that, when done correctly, guarantee a fantastic outcome. Though braising works great on most cuts of meat, this particular recipe pairs two of my favorite flavors: the mild earthiness of lamb and the fruity sweetness of a nice Syrah. The combination produces a dish elegant enough for breaking out the fine china, yet hearty enough to eat by the fireside on chilly winter nights. **SERVES 4**

GREMOLATA

¾ cup flat-leaf parsley, chopped

2 garlic cloves, minced

1 tablespoon lemon zest, finely grated

1 tablespoon fresh mint, finely minced

LAMB SHANKS

4 bone-in lamb shanks, trimmed ½ inch from smaller end

¼ cup olive oil, divided

Coarse salt

Freshly ground black pepper

2 tablespoons all-purpose flour

4 anchovies, diced, plus oil from container

1 large carrot, peeled and diced

2 celery ribs, diced

1 large yellow onion, diced

½ cup fruity red wine, such as a Syrah

2 tablespoons fresh rosemary, finely diced

1 tablespoon fresh thyme, finely diced

2 tablespoons garlic cloves, chopped or smashed

2 cups canned diced tomatoes, drained

2 tablespoons chopped flat-leaf parsley

1 bay leaf

4 cups chicken broth

Mashed potatoes, polenta, or navy beans, for serving

CONTINUED ON NEXT PAGE

MAKE GREMOLATA

Combine all ingredients in a small bowl and mix well. Cover and store in a dry place.

MAKE LAMB SHANKS

Preheat oven to 275°F. Rub shanks with olive oil and season liberally with salt and pepper. Dust with flour to lightly cover meat.

Heat 2 tablespoons olive oil in a Dutch oven over medium-high heat. Add shanks to pot, making sure not to crowd, and sear 3 to 4 minutes per side until crispy brown. Cook in batches if necessary. Remove shanks and set aside.

Reduce heat to medium and add anchovy oil (add anchovies later), carrot, celery, and onion. Sauté until onion is just translucent, about 5 minutes.

Increase heat to high and add wine. Using a wooden spoon, deglaze pot until wine reduces by half, about 5 minutes, stirring and scraping up any browned bits from the bottom of the pot (when they dissolve in the cooking liquid they enrich the entire dish greatly).

Reduce heat to medium and add rosemary, thyme, garlic, and anchovies to vegetable mixture; sauté 3 minutes.

Add tomatoes, parsley, bay leaf, and chicken broth. Simmer 5 minutes and remove from heat.

Add shanks to vegetable mixture, coating each with the liquid but not covering them completely. Remove some of the liquid if necessary so that the liquid covers about 80 percent of shanks. Reserve any liquid removed.

Cover tightly and roast for 3 hours, basting every 30 minutes after the first hour.

Uncover and continue to roast until meat is fork-wtender (30 to 45 minutes). Remove from oven.

Remove shanks and place on a plate; cover with foil. Remove vegetables and place in a bowl; cover with foil. Keep both warm. Spoon away any fat floating in the sauce and add reserved sauce if any was removed. (See Tip below.)

Place the Dutch oven on a burner, bring sauce to a boil, then immediately reduce heat to medium and allow to cook, uncovered, for 30 minutes to reduce and thicken sauce. Stir from time to time, reducing the heat if the hard boil continues.

TO SERVE

Place each shank in a rimmed plate or shallow bowl over mashed potatoes, polenta, or navy beans. Spoon vegetables over and around meat and top with thickened sauce. Season to taste with salt and pepper.

Sprinkle with gremolata and serve immediately with crusty bread.

TIP

For best results, refrigerate the shanks and vegetables after roasting and finish the dish the next day. Sitting overnight allows the flavors to seep out of each herb, spice, veggie, and shank and meld together—a fancy way of saying it will taste a whole lot better. If you go this route, on the day of serving, reduce the sauce as described in the last step, then bake the covered shanks and vegetables at 250°F until warmed through.

Jeff, John, Sarah, and Kristin
in South Beach at the Wine & Food Festival

ST. LOUIS RIBS

EACH TYPE OF MEAT served at the Smokehouse is cooked in a manner that reflects the best style I found during many years of traveling throughout the country. Whereas my pulled pork comes from Alabama and my brisket goes back to Texas, the best ribs I came across were in North Carolina. The combination of apple and pork is good on it own, but the finish with the sweetness of the honey and brown sugar is a treat you don't want to miss. **SERVES 2**

INGREDIENTS

1 full rack of St. Louis-style ribs (about 4 pounds)

2 tablespoons All-Purpose Rub (page 25)

2 cups apple juice, poured into a squirt bottle

2 tablespoons light brown sugar

2 tablespoons honey

¼ cup All-Purpose BBQ Sauce (page 25)

PREPARE SMOKER

Soak wood for 1 hour before smoking.

Light charcoal and allow to burn to a white ash.

Place soaked hickory on top of hot coals and allow the temperature to settle at 225°F.

COOK RIBS

Remove membrane on underside of rack of ribs (or score along the length of the rack with a knife, taking care not to puncture the meat).

Apply rub evenly over top of ribs. Place in smoker and cover. Check and replace wood and coal every hour to maintain a constant temperature.

After 2 hours, begin to spray the ribs with apple juice every 30 minutes

Continue smoking and spraying ribs for another 1½ hours, until the meat turns a dark brown and begins to pull back from the ends of the rib so ¼ to ½ inch of the bone is exposed and meat is tender to touch.

Remove ribs from smoker. Spray with apple juice and sprinkle top with brown sugar and honey, then wrap tightly in aluminum foil.

RIB FACTS

Just as baby back ribs have nothing to do with piglets, St. Louis ribs have nothing to do with St. Louis. They're the trimmed-up version of a sparerib after the tips and flap have been cut off (called a square cut). They wrap around the belly of the pig on the bottom of the rib cage, whereas the baby backs wrap the loin where the rib cage meets the spine. I serve St. Louie's exclusively at the Smokehouse because I like the flavor that the moist bacon fat provides, plus my guests appreciate the additional amount of meat on the larger rib.

Place ribs back in smoker for 30 minutes.

Remove ribs from smoker and keep wrapped until ready to serve. If longer than 30 minutes, place ribs in an empty cooler and close lid tight to preserve heat.

FINISH RIBS

Just before serving, heat a gas grill to high. Remove ribs from wrapping and drizzle with BBQ sauce. Place ribs on hot grill, bottom side down, for 3 minutes. Flip only once, and grill the top side for another 3 minutes, until meat is slightly charred and sugar from the BBQ sauce has caramelized.

SMOKED LEG OF LAMB

AS A COOK. I often go through phases of intrigue with a particular ingredient or cooking style. I become obsessed in researching methods, styles, combinations, and recipes in an effort to create a new recipe with my personal spin. Ultimately, I came to appreciate that the classic combination of basil, rosemary, and garlic with lamb is as pleasing today as it was centuries ago. The nuance of hickory-laced smoke adds a buttery sweet flavor that helps balance the otherwise rich and acidic flavors. **SERVES 6 TO 8**

INGREDIENTS

10 basil leaves

10 garlic cloves, peeled

1 (5- to 6-pound) leg of lamb

¼ cup olive oil

1 tablespoon coarse salt

1 tablespoon freshly ground black pepper

1 tablespoon fresh rosemary, chopped

METHOD

Preheat smoker to 225°F using fresh (or moist) hickory wood.

Using a small knife, make 10 small holes evenly around the leg of lamb. Place a piece of fresh basil above each hole and press it in using a whole clove of garlic.

Whisk together olive oil, salt, pepper, and rosemary; rub lamb with mixture.

Smoke 2 to 3 hours at 225°F or until internal temperature reaches 145°F.

TIP

Smoking large cuts with the bone-in is always preferred because it allows the marrow to seep out during the cooking to drive both flavor and moisture to the meat. However, if using a deboned leg of lamb, leave the fishnet stringing on to help hold the lamb together while smoking. If it doesn't come with the stringing, tie the meat up using kitchen string.

COWBOY PORK CHOPS WITH SOY-HONEY GLAZE

I LOVE SEEING a bone-in, double-cut pork chop coming off a sizzling grill boasting of charred crisscross diamonds while juices slowly ooze down its side. But making sure this lean cut yields juicy perfection and not a chalk-dry hunk of meat can prove to be a challenge. Producing a succulent chop requires some special attention to deal with its density and lack of fat. A combination of four techniques (brining, grilling, smoking, and saucing) produces the desired moist meat while bringing together layers of complementary flavors and textures. The process requires a bit of work, but it's well worth the effort in order to consistently produce a juicy yet lean pork chop. **SERVES 4**

PORK CHOPS/BRINE

4 (14-ounce) bone-in, double-cut (thick) pork chops

1 cup salt

1 cup brown sugar

2 bay leaves

4 cups water

½ cup apple juice

½ cup soy sauce

1 cup maple syrup

MILANESE SOY-HONEY GLAZE

2 tablespoons canola oil

1 large shallot, thinly sliced

Pinch of red pepper flakes

½ teaspoon granulated garlic

1 teaspoon ground ginger

1 tablespoon chopped scallions

1 tablespoon rice wine vinegar

½ cup honey

½ cup apple juice

½ cup soy sauce

½ cup brown sugar

1 tablespoon cornstarch

1 tablespoon cold water

2 tablespoons freshly chopped cilantro

Pinch of coarse salt and freshly ground black pepper

CONTINUED

MAKE PORK CHOPS

Combine all ingredients in a bowl or pan large enough to hold pork chops. Cover and brine for 24 hours.

Remove pork chops from brine and smoke over hickory at 225°F until internal temperature is 145°F.

Remove from smoker and allow to cool.

MAKE GLAZE

Heat oil in a small saucepan over medium heat. Add shallot and cook until soft, about 5 minutes. Stir in red pepper flakes and cook for 30 seconds. Add garlic, ginger, and scallions and cook for 30 seconds.

Loosen bits from bottom of pan with rice wine vinegar. Stir in honey, apple juice, soy sauce, and brown sugar; bring to a simmer.

Mix together cornstarch and water; whisk into simmering liquid. Stir in cilantro. Remove from heat and season with salt and pepper.

Transfer to a bowl and keep at room temperature. If made in advance, reheat and thin with a little water.

TO SERVE

Brush chops with glaze. Put chops on a hot grill and sear until grill marks form. To make perfect "diamond" marks, place at a 45-degree angle for 90 seconds. Turn chop to opposing 45-degree angle and grill for 90 seconds more. Flip and grill for 90 seconds. Then turn chop to opposing 45-degree angle and grill for 90 seconds.

Remove from grill, tent with foil, and allow to rest for 10 minutes.

Ladle remaining sauce over chops and serve warm. The pork chops serve well with grilled slices of pineapple brushed with the glaze and a jasmine rice pilaf.

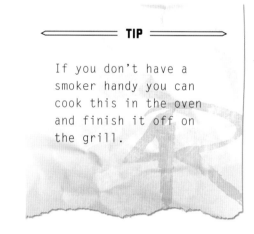

TIP

If you don't have a smoker handy you can cook this in the oven and finish it off on the grill.

POULTRY AND FISH

BUTTERMILK FRIED CHICKEN

RANKING HIGH NEXT TO BBQ is my love for fried chicken. When done right, the crunch of the salty-spicy crust combined with the moist-velvety flavor of chicken is hard to beat. Growing up in Jacksonville, I remember many Sunday family meals at Beach Road Chicken Dinners, a family-owned, home-style diner that's been around since 1939. It remains to this day my favorite place to go for fried chicken. Perhaps it's the chicken or maybe it's the memory of a happy time, but I just can't get enough of the little place when I'm in town. **SERVES 8 TO 12**

2 chickens, each cut into 8 pieces

3 cups corn or canola oil, for frying

BUTTERMILK BRINE

1 quart buttermilk

6 cloves garlic, smashed

2/3 cup hot sauce (such as Texas Pete or Crystal)

1 teaspoon coarsely ground black pepper

3 sprigs rosemary

SEASONED FLOUR

4 cups all-purpose flour

4 tablespoons coarse salt

4 tablespoons coarsely ground black pepper

1 teaspoon granulated garlic

1 teaspoon onion powder

1 teaspoon cayenne pepper

METHOD

Combine brine ingredients in a bowl large enough to hold all of the chicken. Submerge chicken in brine, cover and refrigerate for at least 24 hours, up to 48 hours.

Sift together flour, salt, pepper, garlic, onion powder, and cayenne. Place in a shallow pan for dredging chicken.

Heat oil to 350°F in a cast-iron pan and maintain temperature while fying all of the chicken.

Preheat oven to 350°F.

Drain chicken in colander. Do not rinse.

Dredge one piece of chicken at a time in flour, shaking off excess.

Place chicken, skin side down, in pan and fry until golden brown, about 4 minutes each side for white meat and 5 minutes each side for dark meat. Internal temperature should be around 165°F.

Remove from pan and place on a cookie cooling rack over a sheet pan. Place chicken, rack, and pan in oven and bake for 10 minutes, or until skin is crispy.

TIP

Despite all you've read, resist the urge to double dredge unless you want to taste more crust than chicken.

As a general rule, you can't have enough pepper in fried chicken. Don't be afraid of giving the seasoned flour an extra shake or two.

SMOKED SALMON

GROWING UP IN TEXAS in a family of hunters, my wife, Monica, ate her fair share of venison. She remembers her mom soaking the venison in milk before cooking to help mellow the otherwise "gamey" flavor. With hopes of doing the same to the "fishy" flavor of salmon, she employed this technique to a fillet one night for dinner. The harsh fishy flavor decreased significantly, allowing the herbs and spices to take center stage along with the salmon flesh that had consequently turned smooth and silky. It's not quite clear how dairy products accomplish this, but an accepted explanation is that the calcium activates enzymes in meat that break down proteins, similar to the way aging tenderizes meat. Regardless of the reason, the kids ate fish for dinner without complaining ... and that's a good enough reason for me!

Rubbed with a combination of cumin and brown sugar, the unique flavors became more pronounced while the salmon, laced with a distinct hickory flavor, turns smooth and silky. **SERVES 6**

INGREDIENTS

2 large salmon fillets or sides, pin bones removed (about 3 pounds)

½ gallon whole milk

¾ cup coarse salt

1 cup brown sugar

2 teaspoons cumin

3 teaspoons coarsely ground black pepper

METHOD

Place salmon skin-side up in a glass baking dish or other container large enough for the salmon to lay flat. Pour milk into dish until salmon is covered and allow to soak for 2 hours, refrigerated.

While salmon is soaking, prepare smoker using soaked hickory chips. If using a smoker where the heat is directly under the fish, place a small pan of water on the grate above the coals and below fish. Work with the vents of the smoker until the temperature settles in at 225°F.

In a separate bowl, combine salt, brown sugar, cumin, and black pepper. Stir until combined, cover, and set aside.

Gently remove salmon from milk and pat dry with paper towels. Evenly spread flesh side of salmon with rub and gently work into fish. Place on foil.

Place foil and fish in the smoker directly above the water pan and smoke at 225°F until thickest part registers 130°F, 30 to 40 minutes.

Remove from foil, wrap, and refrigerate. Once cool, remove skin and any gray flesh before serving.

SMOKED CHICKEN POTPIE WITH CHEDDAR BUTTERMILK BISCONES

FEW DISHES CONVEY comfort more than the traditional potpie. Though I didn't come to realize that all potpies didn't come frozen and weren't all microwavable until later in life, my affinity for this hearty home-style dish goes back to my youth and provokes cherished memories just the same.

Full disclosure to all you potpie traditionalists: I failed home economics in high school for the single reason of refusing to eat green peas, and, for the record, my disdain for them has grown over the years. So I substitute green beans, which happen to give the dish a lot more substance.

Despite these slight tweaks on tradition, it's still a dish that warms the heart and tastes like home.

SERVES 10

BUTTERMILK BISCONES

1½ cups all-purpose flour, plus extra for dusting

1½ cups cake flour (not self-rising)

2 tablespoons sugar

2 tablespoons baking powder

¾ teaspoon coarse salt

¼ teaspoon ground cardamom

2 sticks butter, cut into small cubes

1½ cups buttermilk

1 cup cheddar cheese, shredded

EGG WASH

1 jumbo or extra-large egg

1 tablespoon milk

Pinch of salt

SMOKED CHICKEN POTPIE

12 tablespoons butter (1½ sticks), divided, room temperature

1 cup Vidalia onion, finely chopped

2 tablespoons garlic, finely chopped

5 cups chicken broth

2 cups carrots, shredded

1 cup celery, chopped

1½ tablespoons coarse salt

1½ tablespoons coarsely ground black pepper

1½ cups heavy cream, room temperature

½ cup all-purpose flour

1 whole smoked chicken, deboned and cut into bite-size pieces (about 4-5 cups)

2 cups grilled corn

2 cups Southern Green Beans (page 194)

1 tablespoon fresh thyme

1 tablespoon fresh sage

¼ teaspoon cayenne pepper

Coarse salt and freshly ground black pepper, to taste

CONTINUED

MAKE BISCONES

Combine flours, sugar, baking powder, salt, and cardamom in a medium-size mixing bowl.

Add butter and cut in with a pastry fork. Place all ingredients in a food processor fitted with a pastry blade. Pulse carefully until mixture forms small lumps and pea-size clusters. Do not overprocess.

Return flour mixture to mixing bowl. Gradually add buttermilk and gently fold in cheese until mixture is soft yet thick. Add more buttermilk if needed to make mixture moist and sticky.

Gently pat down biscuit mixture in bowl. Dust very lightly with all-purpose flour and refrigerate until ready to assemble potpie.

MAKE EGG WASH

Crack egg into bowl. Add milk and salt. Combine thoroughly.

MAKE CHICKEN POTPIE

Melt 4 tablespoons butter in a large saucepan. Add onion and garlic and sauté about 5 minutes.

Add chicken broth, carrots, celery, salt, and pepper to saucepan and simmer for 8 to 10 minutes.

Add heavy cream. Raise heat to medium and cook until vegetables are soft, about 10 minutes.

In a bowl, cut remaining 8 tablespoons butter into flour to make a paste.

Lower temperature under the saucepan and whisk flour paste slowly into sauce. Mix thoroughly until thickened.

Add chicken, corn, green beans, thyme, sage, and cayenne to mixture. Simmer until thick.

ASSEMBLE

Preheat oven to 450°F.

Lightly grease a 9-by-13-inch baking pan. Transfer potpie mixture to baking dish.

Using a lightly greased ice-cream scoop or ¼ cup measure, cover mixture with 10 buttermilk biscuits. Brush biscuits with egg wash.

Bake for 15 to 20 minutes or until biscuits are golden brown, turning pan about halfway through. Let stand 5 minutes before serving.

BACON-WRAPPED SCALLOPS WITH CRANBERRY CHILI DIPPING SAUCE

THIS RECIPE WAS inspired by Ray Lampe, aka Dr. BBQ, and his book *Dr. BBQ's Big-Time Barbecue Road Trip!* What I love about the way Ray cooks is how he succeeds in combining multiple tastes and sensations in one dish. Here you have the spicy-sweet sauce atop the velvety scallops with a crunch of bacon. A real winner. **MAKES 12**

CRANBERRY CHILI DIPPING SAUCE

- 1 cup cranberry jelly
- 4 tablespoons chili sauce
- 3 tablespoons soy sauce
- 1 teaspoon ground ginger
- 3 tablespoons sriracha
- 1 teaspoon lime juice
- 1 teaspoon lemon juice
- 1 teaspoon garlic, minced
- 1 tablespoon fresh basil, chopped
- 2 tablespoons brown sugar
- 2 tablespoons molasses

SCALLOPS

- 6 slices hickory-smoked bacon
- 12 large sea scallops
- 12 bamboo skewers, soaked in water for 1 hour

MAKE DIPPING SAUCE

Mix all ingredients in a small bowl. Let sit at room temperature for 30 minutes.

MAKE SCALLOPS

Halve bacon slices and sauté over medium heat until transparent but not crisp. Wrap edge of each scallop with a slice of bacon; secure with skewer. Place scallops in a large, shallow, nonreactive bowl. Pour sauce over scallops and refrigerate for 30 minutes to 1 hour.

Remove scallops and set aside. Heat remaining sauce in a pan over medium-high heat until reduced by half, about 5 minutes.

Heat grill to medium-high. Grill scallops until cooked through, about 3 minutes each side, brushing with sauce while grilling. Serve hot scallops with sauce.

John and Ray Lampe at South Beach Wine & Food Festival

PHOTO BY MICHAEL PISARRI

SMOKED CHICKEN

BECAUSE CHICKEN IS such a lean meat, it has the tendency to dry out quicker than other, fattier meats and thus benefits greatly from brining. The salty brine solution interacts with the proteins in the meat to draw in and retain water in the cells. Though some water is lost while cooking, enough is retained to protect the chicken from drying out. Brining also provides the means to drive seasoning to the center of the meat versus just the surface, as marinating or rubs do.

As opposed to the Smoker's Oath to cook "low and slow," chicken benefits from a faster smoke at a higher temperature. The heat causes the skin to crisp, creating an outer barrier to hold and protect the moisture in the meat. Conversely, smoking at the traditional lower temperature has a tendency to produce a rubberlike skin and chalky meat. A quick flash on the grill provides a nice char and caramelizes the BBQ sauce to round out this wonderfully fowl dish. **SERVES 4**

INGREDIENTS

4-pound whole chicken, thawed

1 gallon water (enough to completely submerge chicken)

¾ cup salt

1 cup sugar

1 tablespoon coarsely ground black pepper

1 tablespoon cayenne

¼ cup All-Purpose Rub (page 25)

4 tablespoons All-Purpose BBQ sauce (page 25)

BRINE CHICKEN

Bring water to a boil in a pot large enough to hold the water and chicken. Add sugar and salt, stirring to completely dissolve. Remove from heat, stir in pepper and cayenne, and allow to cool (or add ice) to avoid cooking the chicken. Submerge chicken in brine and refrigerate for 10 to 12 hours.

PREPARE SMOKER

Soak hickory chips or chunks for 1 hour before smoking. Soaking will allow the wood to smolder and smoke for longer periods of time vs catching on fire and quickly burning up.

Light charcoal and allow to burn to a white ash

Place soaked wood on top of hot coals and adjust smoker vents to settle the temperature in at 305°F

SMOKE CHICKEN

Remove chicken from brine and pat dry with a paper towel.

Coat chicken inside and outside with rub seasoning. Separate skin from breast of chicken by inserting your fingers between the two, and sprinkle rub in the opening.

Place seasoned chicken in smoker away from direct heat of coals. If indirect heat is not an option, place a small pan of water (or beer) between the chicken and the hot coals. Close smoker lid and begin smoking.

Check the smoker every hour to ensure the temperature is holding and that wood chips have not burned completely. Add more charcoal and wood as necessary.

Continue smoking until a meat thermometer stuck in the deepest part of the thigh registers 160°F. The cooking time for smoked chicken at this temperature is about 2 to 3 hours but will vary depending on the size of the bird.

Remove chicken from smoker, tent with foil to keep warm. Cut bird in half or quarters if desired.

Heat a gas or charcoal grill to high. Brush one side of the smoked chicken with BBQ sauce and place sauce side down, directly over the hot part of the grill, for 1 to 2 minutes to char.

Brush sauce on top side of chicken, flip and repeat char for another 1 to 2 minutes.

Remove from grill, tent with foil, and let rest 10 minutes before serving.

STACKED CHICKEN ENCHILADAS VERDE

A CONVERSATION STARTER. this is a fun and beautiful way to present one of my favorite Mexican dishes. I was introduced to it at Joe T Garcia's in Fort Worth while living in Texas during the late 1990s. I kick up the heat in the salsa verde a bit more than the traditional version to offset the cool tones of the sour cream; however, you can dial it back by simply reducing the amount of jalapeños.
SERVES 4

PICO DE GALLO
Makes 2 cups

2 whole jalapeños

5 Roma tomatoes

1 medium sweet onion

1 bunch cilantro, roughly chopped, stems removed

Juice of 1 medium lime

Coarse salt, to taste

SALSA VERDE

3 pounds tomatillos, husked and rinsed

2 whole fresh jalapeños, stems removed

3 garlic cloves, peeled

1 large sweet onion, coarsely chopped

2 whole serrano chiles, stems removed

1½ teaspoons ground cumin

2 teaspoons coarse salt

2 bunches cilantro, thick stems removed

¾ cup loosely packed Italian parsley

2 teaspoons fresh lime juice

¼ cup sour cream

ENCHILADAS

1 whole roasted or smoked chicken, at least 2 cups shredded

½ cup heavy cream or half-and-half

1 teaspoon ground cumin

½ cup fresh cilantro, finely chopped, divided

2 large poblano chiles

1 cup sour cream, plus more for serving

6 tablespoons vegetable oil, divided

12 (6-inch) corn or flour tortillas

3 cups Mexican cheese, shredded

FOR SERVING

¼ cup pickled jalapeños

Sour cream (optional)

MAKE PICO DE GALLO

For less heat, remove seeds and veins from jalapeños.

Finely dice tomato, onion, and jalapeños, and combine with cilantro in a mixing bowl. Stir in lime juice and salt. Refrigerate at least 2 hours before serving (preferably overnight).

MAKE SALSA VERDE

Place tomatillos and jalapeños in a large saucepan and cover with water. Bring to a boil, reduce heat, and simmer for 15 minutes. Remove from heat, let stand for 15 minutes, then drain.

Pour mixture into a food processor, add garlic and onions, and pulse 4 to 5 times to course chop.

Add remaining ingredients except for sour cream and blend until chunky.

Add sour cream and pulse a few times to blend well.

To thicken slightly, if desired, pour into saucepan and simmer for 10 minutes.

MAKE ENCHILADAS

While chicken is warm, remove skin and shred meat using hands or two forks. Should yield about 2 cups of shredded meat. Discard bones and skin.

Stir together chicken, cream, cumin, and ¼ cup cilantro in a mixing bowl. Cover and marinate while preparing rest of ingredients. (Refrigerate if longer than 30 minutes.)

Char poblanos over a gas flame or under an oven broiler until blackened. Remove from heat and enclose in a paper bag for 10 minutes. Peel charred skin, remove seeds, and cut into 2-by-½-inch-wide strips. Set aside.

Whisk together remaining cilantro and sour cream in a small mixing bowl.

Heat 2 tablespoons oil in a skillet over medium heat. Using tongs, fry 1 tortilla at a time for about 15 seconds on each side or until slightly softened. Don't overcook, or tortillas will harden. Transfer to paper towels and keep warm. Add oil as needed and fry remaining tortillas.

Preheat oven to 375°F.

For each stack, spoon 2 tablespoons salsa verde on bottom of baking dish large enough to hold 4 stacks.

Place 1 tortilla on salsa verde, cover with ¼ cup chicken, 3 to 4 strips poblano, and 1 tablespoon of sour cream spread. Repeat. Finish each stack with a tortilla, salsa verde, sour cream spread, and shredded cheese.

Bake in middle rack until cheese is bubbly and golden, about 35 minutes.

TO SERVE

Top with remaining cilantro and pico de gallo. Serve hot with sour cream and pickled jalapeños.

POULTRY AND FISH

THANKSGIVING

THANKSGIVING IS THE BUSIEST TIME of the year at the Smokehouse. Weeks of brining, seasoning, and smoking go into nearly a thousand smoked turkeys being sold the day before Thanksgiving. While everything might appear calm and collected to our guests, behind the scenes it is "turkey madness," the culmination of countless hours of work and many sleepless nights. When Thanksgiving Day itself arrives, the last thing I want to do is cook. This is the one day of the year that I happily turn over my knife and apron.

We have a time-honored tradition on Thanksgiving that I treasure greatly. We drive to Jacksonville for the annual extended-family gathering. Welcoming us into their home, my Uncle John and Aunt Sarah create the meal that has become synonymous with the holiday. Uncle John smokes the turkey (which by the way, is better than mine) and bakes the apple pie, while Aunt Sarah orchestrates a symphony of green bean casserole, turkey dressing, sweet potatoes, and mashed potatoes like no other. We give thanks for the many blessings in our lives and the fellowship with those we love and enjoy the feast until groans of joy outweigh the sounds of forks and knives.

When not another bite can be eaten, the clan takes off to enjoy our traditional stroll through the beautiful oak-lined streets along the St. John's River in San Marco where we grew up. As babies are born and siblings juggle other family commitments, the group changes from year to hear. However, there is no other single day in our family that so many generations come together to enjoy each other's company.

Few things say family to me more than this one day of the year. I pray we're always so fortunate to enjoy such a blessing in our lives.

SMOKED TURKEY

BRINING IS KEY to creating a perfect Thanksgiving bird, and our Turkey Brine calls for some of the savory elements we associate with the holiday. Beyond that, the fresher the turkey the better. And spraying the turkey with apple juice adds to the sweetness and moisture of the final product.
SERVES 10–12

TURKEY BRINE

1½ cups kosher salt

1 ¼ cups brown sugar

6 sprigs thyme (or 3 teaspoons dried)

6 sprigs sage (or 3 teaspoons dried)

6 sprigs rosemary (or 3 teaspoons dried)

2 apples, quartered

2 oranges, quartered

3 teaspoons black peppercorns

1½ gallons (6 quarts) water, apple juice or apple cider (or a combination of these)

TURKEY

1 (18- to 22-pound) turkey, thawed and cleaned (smaller turkeys will work just as well)

½ cup vegetable oil

¼ cup kosher salt

¼ cup black pepper

1 teaspoon ground sage

1 teaspoon ground thyme

3 cups apple juice in a squirt bottle

BOURBON GLAZE

Bones from 3 smoked chickens or one large smoked turkey, picked free of meat

1 onion, quartered

2 stalks celery, halved

Salt and pepper to taste

1 gallon water

½ cup bourbon

½ cup All-Purpose BBQ sauce (page 25)

*Option: If you don't want to make the broth from scratch, you can substitute 1½ cups canned chicken broth for the first 5 ingredients in this recipe.

BRINE AND SMOKE TURKEY

Combine all ingredients except fruit and herbs in a non-reactive pot and stir until mixed completely. Add fruit and herbs and keep cold. Can be prepared up to 24 hours in advance.

Submerge turkey completely in brine and allow to soak overnight in a refrigerator or in a cooler with ice packs careful to not allow the temperature of water to rise above 41°F.

Light charcoal in smoker, cover and allow to reach and rest at 225°F.

Remove turkey from brine and pat dry with paper towel. Save vegetables and herbs from brine. Coat outside of turkey with oil and rub entire bird with salt, pepper, ground sage and a touch of ground thyme covering the inside cavity as well. Once rubbed, stuff cavity with vegetables and herbs from brine.

Add wood directly on top of hot coals to create a heavy smoke. Place turkey in smoker, cover tightly and monitor temperature of smoker to maintain a constant 225°F, more charcoal as needed. Add wood when initial chunks are burnt so a constant stream of smoke is maintained.

After first hour, then every hour following, spray turkey with apple juice, being careful not to allow the smoker to remain open for any more than necessary. Allow to smoke until the internal temperature of turkey thighs reache 155°F (roughly 4 to 6 hours).

MAKE BOURBON GLAZE

You can make this in advance or while turkey is smoking. Add poultry bones, vegetables and spices to water and bring to a boil. Reduce heat and let simmer uncovered for 3 hours. Pour broth through a strainer, taking care to capture all the liquid. Discard bones and vegetables. Pour broth back into pot, bring to boil and reduce by another ⅓ to approximately 4 cups.

In a separate pan, add bourbon and bring to a fast boil. Lower heat to medium and allow bourbon to reduce to ¼ cup, about 5 minutes. Add All-Purpose BBQ sauce and 1½ cups of the broth. Bring to a boil. Reduce heat to medium-low and continue cooking for 45 minutes, until glaze is thick enough to coat the back of a spoon.

TO SERVE

Remove turkey from smoker, place in shallow roasting pan and cover with foil or saran wrap. Allow meat to rest for 30 minutes or up to an hour. Slice and serve with warm bourbon glaze.

SOUTHERN GREEN BEANS

SERVES 6

INGREDIENTS

1 smoked ham hock, about 8 ounces

8 ounces salt pork, cubed (or 6 slices thick-cut bacon)

1 cup diced onion

4½ cups chicken broth, plus more if needed

32 ounces frozen green beans

1½ tablespoons coarse salt

1½ tablespoons freshly ground black pepper

1 tablespoon sugar

2 tablespoons unsalted butter

METHOD

Preheat oven to 350°F and bake ham hock for 10 minutes, until it begins to release its juices.

Remove from oven and set aside, taking care to reserve juices in the baking pan.

Meanwhile, sauté salt pork over medium-high heat in a Dutch oven or large skillet until it begins to release grease and the fat becomes slightly translucent, about 5 minutes.

Add onion and continue cooking until onion is translucent, about 5 minutes.

Add chicken broth, stirring to loosen browned bits from bottom of pan. Bring to a rolling boil.

Add beans, salt, pepper, sugar, and ham hock.

Reduce heat to a simmer, cover and cook for 2½ hours. Add more chicken broth as needed.

Add butter and continue to cook uncovered for 30 minutes, or until beans are dark green and tender.

BAKED GRUYÈRE MASHED POTATOES

THIS RECIPE WAS inspired by Monica's simpler but just as good home version (see Tip below), and it was whipped up to accompany the Coffee-Rubbed Cowboy Rib Eye Steak we served at a pop-up event held to test our Cowboy Kitchen concept. The distinct sharp flavor of the Gruyère provides a nice contrast to the sweeter undertones of the coffee rub while marrying well with the silky, buttery potatoes. **SERVES 10**

INGREDIENTS

5 pounds russet or Yukon gold potatoes

2 sticks plus ¼ stick unsalted butter

1 cup warm half-and-half

½ cup shredded Gruyère cheese

4 ounces cream cheese, softened

2 teaspoons kosher salt

1 teaspoon freshly ground black pepper

METHOD

Preheat oven to 350°F.

Peel potatoes, leaving about 50 percent of skin on. Cut into 2- to 3-inch chunks. Cook in boiling, lightly salted water until fork tender, 20 to 25 minutes. Drain and let air dry for 3 to 5 minutes.

While potatoes are warm, hand mash to desired consistency and transfer to a mixing bowl. Using a mixer or a handheld beater, mix at medium speed for about 2 minutes to fluff potatoes.

Add 2 sticks butter, warm half-and-half, cream cheese, salt, and pepper and continue to mix for another minute to combine.

Fold in Gruyère cheese and add additional salt and pepper to taste.

Spread the potatoes into a generously buttered 4-quart baking dish. Top with remaining butter cut into pats and bake for 25 minutes, until butter is melted and potatoes are warmed through.

TIP

For an easier home version, omit the Gruyère and cream cheese and don't worry about baking it. The butter, salt, and warm half-and-half pack enough punch to warm the heart ... and fill the tummy!

You also can substitute Parmesan cheese for the Gruyère when serving with a tomato-based dish such as Osso Bucco or Braised Lamb Shanks.

PROSCIUTTO BRUSSELS SPROUTS

SERVES 4

INGREDIENTS

1 pound fresh Brussels sprouts

4 slices bacon, roughly chopped

¾ cup diced white onion

1 tablespoon minced garlic

2 tablespoons brown sugar

2 ounces sliced prosciutto, about 4 thin slices, diced

1 teaspoons coarse salt

1 teaspoon freshly ground black pepper

½ teaspoon cayenne pepper

1 tablespoon unsalted butter

METHOD

Cut off ends of Brussels sprouts, pull off any outer yellow leaves, trim and cut in half. Partially cook in a large pot of boiling water, about 3 minutes. Drain and pat dry.

Fry bacon in a skillet over medium heat until crisp; remove bacon, and in same pan sauté onion for 5 to 8 minutes. Add garlic and sauté until golden, about 2 minutes. Add Brussels sprouts and cook until golden brown on the outside, about 5 minutes. Stir in brown sugar to coat. Stir in diced prosciutto and bacon.

Continue cooking until Brussels sprouts are caramelized and just tender, about 10 minutes. Add salt, pepper, and cayenne. Lower heat and add butter to coat Brussels sprouts. Serve hot.

ERIC'S SAUSAGE DRESSING

SERVES 10–12

INGREDIENTS

16-ounce package Jimmy Dean Sage Sausage

8 tablespoons (1 stick) butter

1 cup chopped white onion

1 cup chopped celery

2 tablespoons chopped garlic

1 tablespoon dried sage

½ teaspoon celery salt

2 (14-ounce) cans chicken broth

14-ounce bag cornbread stuffing mix

Coarsely ground black pepper, to taste

METHOD

Preheat oven to 350°F.

Thoroughly cook sausage in a large saucepan. Discard grease and wipe pan clean.

Melt butter in same saucepan and add onion, celery, garlic, sage, and celery salt. Sauté until vegetables are translucent, about 6 to 8 minutes.

Add chicken broth, cooked sausage, and stuffing mix. Blend all ingredients until stuffing is thoroughly moistened. Taste and season with pepper if needed.

Lightly grease 9-by-13-inch baking pan. Place stuffing in pan and bake in oven for 50 to 60 minutes. Cover with foil and keep warm until ready to serve.

*A special thanks to my good friends Eric and Toni Scott

SWEET POTATO CASSEROLE

SERVES 8

INGREDIENTS

6 cups mashed sweet potatoes, about 2 pounds fresh

1 cup brown sugar

¼ cup melted butter

1 (14-ounce) can sweetened condensed milk

2 eggs, beaten

½ teaspoon salt

½ teaspoon vanilla

¼ teaspoon cinnamon

¼ teaspoon ginger

¼ teaspoon nutmeg

1 cup pecans, coarsely chopped

METHOD

Preheat oven to 350°F.

Combine all ingredients except pecans in a 9-by-13-inch casserole dish. Sprinkle with pecans.

Bake 35 minutes or until it slightly puffs. Serve warm.

RED VELVET CAKE

FAR AND AWAY the most popular dessert in our Sweet Shop, Red Velvet Cake's true origin is as disputed as the "right" way to make it. One popular myth has it originating at the Waldorf-Astoria Hotel in New York City where a guest wrote to request the recipe. It arrived, along with a bill for $300 from the Waldorf's chef. The outraged guest reportedly made it a personal mission to share the highly coveted secret with every household across the country. Though this may have very well happened, I like to believe that the origins of this amped-up variation of a devil's food cake come from somewhere below the Mason-Dixon line. In any event, this is our take on the classic, and you're welcome to share it with whomever you like ... at no cost. **MAKES 9-INCH (3-LAYER) CAKE**

RED VELVET CAKE

3¾ cups all-purpose flour

3 cups sugar

4½ tablespoons cocoa powder

1½ teaspoons baking soda

1½ teaspoons salt

3 large eggs

2¼ cups margarine, melted

1½ cups buttermilk

1½ teaspoons vanilla extract

¼ cup plus 2 tablespoons red food coloring

Shredded coconut, for garnish

RED VELVET CAKE ICING

½ pound (two 8-ounce sticks) salted butter, room temperature

8 ounces cream cheese, room temperature

4 cups confectioners' sugar

MAKE CAKE

Preheat oven to 350°F. Grease and flour 3 (9-inch) round cake pans.

Whisk together flour, sugar, cocoa powder, baking soda, and salt in large mixing bowl.

In a separate bowl, mix eggs, melted margarine, buttermilk, vanilla, and red food coloring.

In mixer using whisk attachment, slowly pour wet mixture into flour mixture. Once incorporated, mix on high for 30 seconds.

Divide batter into prepared pans (about 2½ cups per pan). Bake 26 minutes or until cake tester comes out clean.

Remove from oven and cool slightly. Unmold from pans and finish cooling on wire rack. If necessary, slice tops of each cake slightly to achieve uniform size and flat surface for ease in icing.

MAKE ICING

Blend butter and cream cheese until soft and fully combined in a mixer. Slowly add confectioners' sugar, mixing thoroughly. Mix on high speed for about 3 minutes until light and fluffy.

ASSEMBLE

Ice top and sides of one cake, then place second cake on top of iced cake and repeat step. Place third cake on top, making sure to turn over for ease in icing final layer. Garnish with shredded coconut.

COCONUT CREAM PIE

EDGING OUT BANANA CREAM pie by a flake, coconut cream pie is my favorite dessert. To properly honor it, I went to great lengths scouring the country in search of the perfect blend of coconut, custard, and cream. Years of tenacious pie testing seemed to be in vain until I came across a surprisingly simple recipe from Loveless Café, near Nashville, involving the basic technique of baking the custard over a bed of coconut. It proved to be just what I was searching for. After a few tweaks to the recipe, coconut nirvana was at last achieved, proving that true goodness doesn't always come easy but is certainly worth the journey. **MAKES A 10-INCH PIE**

INGREDIENTS

1 (10-inch) baked pie shell

2½ cups shredded coconut, plus 4 tablespoons for garnish

2 cups half-and-half

1¼ cup sugar, divided

3 large eggs

2 teaspoons vanilla extract, divided

2 cups heavy cream

METHOD

Preheat oven to 350°F.

Spread coconut on a rimmed baking sheet and bake, stirring once or twice, until golden, about 10 minutes. Remove from oven and cool.

Increase oven temperature to 375°F. Spread 2½ cups toasted coconut in bottom of baked pie shell and press down gently until coconut slightly sticks to the shell. This will help prevent all of the coconut from floating to the top of the pie. Place pie shell on a baking sheet and set aside.

Whisk together half-and-half, 1 cup sugar, eggs, and 1 teaspoon vanilla; pour over coconut.

Bake about 45 minutes, or until golden and puffy with a firm center. Cool completely before topping.

For topping, combine heavy cream, remaining sugar, and remaining vanilla; whip until stiff peaks form. Spread evenly over pie. Garnish with remaining coconut and chill until ready to serve.

BOURBON PECAN PIE

PECAN PIE IS BELOVED throughout the South due in large part to the abundance of pecan trees and roadside stands selling pee-cans in all variations. Nowadays it's one of those desserts that transcends borders and can be as commonly found in California as Georgia. I don't know for sure where the addition of bourbon got started, but it creates a smooth undertone of flavor that elevates the classic to a whole new level. **MAKE A 9-INCH PIE**

CRUST

6 tablespoons salted butter, room temperature

4 ounces cream cheese, room temperature

1 cup all-purpose flour

FILLING

¾ cup light brown sugar

¾ cup dark brown sugar

4 eggs

2 tablespoons salted butter, melted

1 cup light corn syrup

2 cups toasted pecan halves

2 to 4 tablespoons bourbon (depending on your preference for the strength of the bourbon flavor)

WHIPPED CREAM

1 cup sugar

1 teaspoon vanilla extract

2 cups heavy whipping cream

MAKE CRUST

Process butter, cream cheese, and flour in a food processor until dough just begins to form a ball. Flatten dough into a disk and wrap in plastic wrap. Refrigerate for 30 minutes or overnight.

Rub flour over a rolling pin to prevent sticking. Roll cold dough gently from center to the edge, maintaining a circle shape, rotating and flouring dough to make sure it doesn't stick.

Fold dough in half, place in a 9-inch pie pan and unfold to fit pan.

MAKE FILLING

Preheat oven to 350°F.

Mix together all ingredients in a large bowl. Pour into crust.

Bake for 35 minutes (center of filling should be slightly soft). Transfer to rack and let cool 3 to 4 hours.

ASSEMBLE

For the whipped cream topping, combine all ingredients in a mixer and whip until stiff peaks form. Give each slice of pie a generous dollop.

FUN VARIATIONS

You can add ½ cup of chocolate chips to the filling to make Chocolate Pecan Pie. And you can add 1 tablespoon of bourbon to whipped cream for an extra kick.

KRISPY KREME BREAD PUDDING

EATING A HOT Krispy Kreme doughnut straight off the conveyer belt when the big, red neon sign outside announces the arrival of a fresh batch is an essential rite of passage in the South. Inspired by Paula Deen's version of this recipe, I made a few changes to make it my own and, admittedly, made it way over the top on the decadence scale. **SERVES 8 TO 10**

PUDDING

1 cup sugar

4 tablespoons unsalted butter, softened

2 cups half-and-half

2 eggs

2 teaspoons cinnamon

1 teaspoon vanilla extract

1 8-ounce can crushed pineapple

¾ cup raisins

1 dozen Krispy Kreme doughnuts, cubed

RUM GLAZE

1 stick butter, unsalted

¼ cup half-and-half

2 teaspoons vanilla extract

2 teaspoons rum (Mount Gay preferred)

4 cups confectioners' sugar

MAKE PUDDING

Preheat oven to 350°F. Lightly butter a 13-by-9-inch baking dish.

Combine sugar, butter, half-and-half, and eggs in a large bowl with an electric mixer. Stir in cinnamon and vanilla.

Fold in pineapple, raisins, and doughnuts.

Cover and refrigerate for an hour to allow doughnuts to soak in liquid.

Bake 60 minutes or until center is jelled (but not firm or dry) and bread pudding is puffy and golden.

Make rum glaze while pudding is baking

Puncture top of pudding with a butter knife every ½ inch and pour warm glaze over the top to seep into cuts and cover pudding completely.

MAKE RUM GLAZE

Combine butter, half-and-half, vanilla, and rum in a medium saucepan over low heat; heat until warm.

Whisk confectioners' sugar into mixture until smooth and heat until just bubbling. Remove from heat, set aside, and keep warm.

TIP

The key to good bread pudding is keeping it moist. To ensure a moist pudding, start with a very wet base, almost but not quite runny. And bake the pudding in a water bath (place the pudding baking dish in a larger baking dish filled with water, so that about 80 percent of the outside of the smaller dish is immersed, and place both dishes in the oven). Doing so may require a longer cook time, but it's well worth the wait.

1

CHOCOLATE AWESOMENESS

2
PEANUT BUTTER FLUFF
PUDDING CUPS

3
BANANA DREAM PUDDING

1 CHOCOLATE AWESOMENESS

SERVES 6

PUDDING

¾ cup crumbled chocolate cake, divided

6 tablespoons strong coffee, divided

3 cups prepared chocolate pudding, divided

3 cups whipped cream, divided

6 tablespoons chocolate-toffee bits (such as Heath), divided

6 tablespoons 4R Chocolate Sauce (Recipe follows)

6 tablespoons 4R Caramel Sauce, divided (page 212)

4R CHOCOLATE SAUCE

1⅓ cup unsweetened cocoa

2⅓ cups sugar

2½ cups water

2 teaspoons vanilla extract

1 teaspoon kosher salt

MAKE CHOCOLATE SAUCE

Combine cocoa, sugar, water and salt in small saucepan and bring to boil over medium-high heat. Reduce heat and boil gently for 2 minutes.

Remove from heat and stir in vanilla. Let cool before serving.

MAKE PUDDING

Place 2 tablespoons cake crumbs at the bottom of each serving cup. Drizzle coffee over crumbs.

Top with ½ cup chocolate pudding and ½ cup whipped cream.

Sprinkle with 2 tablespoons toffee chips, then drizzle with 2 tablespoons 4R Chocolate Sauce and 2 tablespoons 4R Caramel Sauce.

2 PEANUT BUTTER FLUFF PUDDING CUPS

MAKES 6 PUDDING CUPS

PEANUT BUTTER FLUFF PUDDING

1¾ cups prepared vanilla pudding

¾ cup creamy peanut butter

¾ cup Marshmallow Fluff

¾ cup crisp rice cereal

¾ cup chocolate-toffee bits (such as Heath)

¾ cup graham cracker crumbs

PUDDING CUPS

1 cup plus 2 tablespoons chocolate sandwich cookies, crushed

Peanut Butter Fluff Pudding

3 cups whipped cream

6 tablespoons chocolate-toffee bits (such as Heath)

3 peanut butter cups (such as Reese's), halved

CONTINUED

MAKE PEANUT BUTTER FLUFF PUDDING

Combine vanilla pudding, peanut butter, and Marshmallow Fluff in a large bowl; beat with an electric mixer until well combined.

Combine crisp rice cereal, crushed chocolate-toffee bits, and graham cracker crumbs in a medium bowl. Fold into pudding mixture until well combined.

MAKE PUDDING CUPS

Place 3 tablespoons crushed chocolate sandwich cookies at the bottom of each serving cup or parfait glass.

Top with ½ cup peanut butter fluff pudding, ½ cup whipped cream, 1 tablespoon crushed chocolate-toffee bits, and half of a peanut butter cup.

3 BANANA DREAM PUDDING CUPS

SERVES 6

BANANA DREAM PUREE

5 large ripe bananas

2 tablespoons sugar

1½ cups vanilla pudding

BANANA DREAM PUDDING CUPS

1 cup graham cracker crumbs

1 tablespoon powdered sugar

1 tablespoon unsalted butter, melted

18 (¼-inch-thick) banana slices

12 tablespoons toffee-chocolate bits, such as Heath, divided

3 cups Banana Dream Puree, divided

1¾ cups freshly whipped cream, divided

6 tablespoons chocolate sauce, divided

6 tablespoons caramel sauce, divided

18 vanilla wafers

MAKE PUREE

Preheat oven to 375°F. Lay bananas, unpeeled, on a baking sheet and bake for 10 to 15 minutes, or until bananas turn dark brown and go soft. Allow bananas to cool before peeling.

Peel bananas and place in the work bowl of a food processor, along with the sugar. Pulse until desired smoothness. I prefer a few chunks for texture but others like it smooth and silky.

Add pudding to bowl and mix by hand until combined. Refrigerate until cold.

MAKE PUDDING CUPS

Combine graham cracker crumbs, powdered sugar, and melted butter in a bowl, and mix until well blended.

In each of 6 glass dishes, place 2 tablespoons graham cracker mixture, then top with 3 banana slices and a tablespoon of toffee-chocolate bits.

Spoon in ½ cup puree, then top with ¼ cup whipped cream.

Sprinkle with 1 tablespoon toffee-chocolate bits, and drizzle with 1 tablespoon chocolate sauce and 1 tablespoon caramel sauce. Refrigerate until ready to serve.

Place 3 vanilla wafers around each rim just before serving.

CARAMEL PECAN CAKE

THIS BEAUTIFUL CAKE speaks to the heart of Southern culture and our love of caramel and pecans ... no matter how you pronounce them. While it might sound like a fairly simple cake, it was tricky finding the right balance of caramel in the icing and filling without going overboard. Since caramel is one of my favorite sweet flavors, the first few times I made this cake I went too heavy on caramel and got in trouble with Amanda Eubanks, our head baker. But after countless caramel negotiations, we came to a compromise that I hope you agree is just the right balance for you caramel lovers out there.

MAKES 1 (9-INCH, 3-LAYER) CAKE

4R CARAMEL SAUCE

- 2 cups heavy cream, room temperature
- 1 teaspoon vanilla extract
- 4 cups water
- 4 cups sugar
- 1 teaspoon fresh lemon juice

CARAMEL PECAN CAKE

- 1½ cups self-rising flour
- 1¼ cups all-purpose flour
- 2 cups sugar
- 1 cup salted butter, room temperature
- 4 large eggs, room temperature
- 1 cup whole milk, room temperature
- 1 cup 4R Caramel Sauce
- 1 cup pecans, toasted, chopped
- 2 teaspoons vanilla

CARAMEL MOUSSE

- 2 cups cold heavy whipping cream
- 1 (3.4-ounce) box vanilla instant pudding mix
- ¼ cup 4R Caramel Sauce

CARAMEL FROSTING

- 1 cup salted butter, room temperature
- 1 cup 4R Caramel Sauce
- 2 pounds confectioners' sugar

MAKE CARAMEL SAUCE

Combine water, sugar, and lemon juice in a large saucepan over low heat; stir until sugar is dissolved. Raise heat to high and bring mixer to boil; do not stir. Boil sugar-water mixture, swirling pan, until it turns golden brown, about 5 to 7 minutes.

Remove from heat; stand back and pour in cream. Mixture will bubble vigorously and caramel will solidify.

Return saucepan over low heat, and simmer, stirring constantly, until caramel dissolves and sauce is smooth, about 2 minutes. Set aside to cool to room temperature, at least 2 hours.

MAKE CAKE

Preheat oven to 350°F. Butter and flour 3 (9-inch) cake pans. Set aside.

Whisk together self-rising flour and all-purpose flour in a large bowl; set aside.

Cream sugar and butter together in a separate large bowl using an electric mixer. Add eggs one at a time, waiting until each egg is incorporated before adding the next.

Alternately add flour and milk, in 3 batches, beginning and ending with flour. Mix until just combined. Fold in caramel, pecans, and vanilla until just combined.

Bake 22 minutes, or until golden.

MAKE MOUSSE

Combine all ingredients in a large bowl. Whip with an electric mixer until stiff peaks form.

MAKE FROSTING

Combine butter and caramel sauce in a large bowl. Whip with electric mixer until combined. Slowly add confectioners' sugar, scraping the bowl often until combined.

Combine heavy cream and vanilla extract in a large measuring cup and set aside.

ASSEMBLE

Place one cake layer on a platter or cake stand. Top with half of caramel mousse, spreading almost to edges.

Place a second cake layer on top, then spread remaining mousse on that layer. Top with third cake layer.

Frost cake with caramel frosting.

DOUBLE CHOCOLATE BREAD PUDDING WITH BACON-AND-HICKORY-CHIP-INFUSED CRÈME ANGLAISE

NOT LONG AFTER the Smokehouse opened we were contacted by *Plate* magazine and asked to submit ideas for a special issue they were doing on unique wood-cooked dishes. Guessing that most folks would respond with traditional smoked or grilled dishes, I popped off something along the lines of "What about incorporating hickory chips into a sauce such as a bacon-flavored crème anglaise and putting it over a chocolate bread pudding?" Now keep in mind, up to this point I hadn't ever made a crème anglaise ... let alone was I able to pronounce it properly. Well, they loved the idea and the pressure was on to create what would become our first ever nationally published recipe! I'm not saying it didn't take a lot of experimenting, with plenty of mistakes along the way. But I think you'll agree that the result speaks for itself.

If using hickory chips is too much to swallow, leave them out, and the sauce will taste just as good.

SERVES 12

BREAD PUDDING

7 slices stale challah bread, sliced 1 inch thick

1 stick unsalted butter, to butter ramekins

3 cups heavy cream

¾ cup sugar

½ cup semisweet chocolate chips

½ cup milk chocolate chips

1 ounce espresso

1 tablespoon vanilla

7 egg yolks, beaten

¼ teaspoon salt

CRÈME ANGLAISE

6 slices bacon, divided

2 tablespoons hickory BBQ pellets or small hickory wood chips

2 cups half-and-half

7 egg yolks

½ teaspoon arrowroot or 1½ teaspoons cornstarch (optional)

⅓ cup sugar

MAKE BREAD PUDDING

Preheat oven to 350°F.

Remove crusts from bread and dice into ½-inch squares.

Place bread cubes into 12 buttered, 5-ounce ramekins, filling about halfway.

Slowly bring heavy cream and sugar to a boil over medium heat in a medium saucepan. Reduce heat to simmer and add semisweet chocolate, milk chocolate, espresso, and vanilla. Whisk until smooth.

Remove from heat; add egg yolks and salt, whisking until incorporated.

Pour chocolate mixture over bread in ramekins, filling to about ¼ inch from the rim. Press bread down firmly until fully covered in chocolate.

Allow to sit for 30 minutes, or cover and refrigerate overnight.

Bake for 30 minutes, or until slightly firm to touch. Remove from oven and cool slightly before serving.

MAKE CRÈME ANGLAISE

Place hickory pellets/wood chips in a bowl and cover with water. Soak for 15 minutes, then strain.

Cook 4 slices bacon in a heavy skillet over medium heat. Once translucent, sprinkle 1 tablespoon of strained pellets/chips evenly over bacon. Continue cooking for about 5 minutes. Do not allow bacon to crisp. Remove from heat.

Meanwhile, slowly bring half-and-half to boil in a small saucepan. Add cooked strips of bacon with pellets/chips to pan. Remove from heat, cover with plastic wrap, and allow to sit for 15 minutes.

In a medium bowl, whisk egg yolks until light in color. Add arrowroot or cornstarch to yolks (optional), whisk to thoroughly incorporate.

Return half-and-half and bacon mixture to heat. Bring to a boil and add sugar. Stir until sugar is dissolved, and remove from heat.

Temper egg yolks by slowly incorporating the half-and-half mixture, whisking constantly. When about 50 percent of half-and-half mixture remains, whisk the balance into yolks. Return to saucepan.

Over low heat, cook and thicken crème until it coats the back of a spoon and reaches 165°F (or 170°F if optional starch is used). Remove from heat.

Through a fine-mesh sieve, strain crème into a bowl placed in an ice bath, which has been prepared in advance. Allow time for all of the crème to seep, pressing down with back of spoon as necessary.

ASSEMBLE

Fry remaining two slices bacon until crispy. Chop into small pieces consistent in size.

Invert each warm bread pudding on a plate. Spoon crème anglaise over pudding. Dust with bacon and serve immediately.

PHOTO BY MELISSA SPILMAN

COCONUT CAKE

Bakers Renee and Amanda

IN HONOR OF my wonderful mother, Teresa, to whom I attribute my love of coconut, it's only fitting to include in our first cookbook her very favorite dessert from our bakery. It only took one bite of Amanda's Coconut Cake, and I knew I had found my head baker. After all, anyone who could make Mom this happy certainly deserved to be the boss in my bakery!

Many thanks to Amanda for sharing her wonderful recipe and to Mom for teaching us an appreciation for such a delicious combination of flavors.

MAKES 1 (9-INCH, 3-LAYER) CAKE

- 1 cup salted butter, room temperature
- 2 cups sugar
- 4 large eggs
- 1½ cups self rising flour
- 1¼ cups all purpose flour
- 1 cup whole milk
- 1½ cups shredded sweetened coconut
- 2 teaspoons vanilla

FROSTING

- 1 (8-ounce) package cream cheese, softened
- 1 cup (2 sticks) salted butter, softened
- 4 cups confectioners' sugar

FOR ASSEMBLY

- 4 cups coconut, shredded

MAKE CAKE

Preheat oven to 350°F. Butter and flour 3 (9-inch) cake pans. Set aside.

Whisk together self-rising flour and all-purpose flour in a large bowl; set aside.

Cream sugar and butter together in a separate large bowl using an electric mixer. Add eggs one at a time, waiting until each egg is incorporated before adding the next.

Alternately add flour and milk, in 3 batches, beginning and ending with flour. Mix until just combined. Fold in coconut and vanilla until just combined.

Divide evenly batter among prepared pans. Bake 22 minutes, or until golden.

MAKE FROSTING

Cream butter and cream cheese in a large bowl with an electric mixer until completely combined. Slowly add confectioners' sugar.

Once sugar is incorporated, mix on high until smooth and fluffy.

ASSEMBLE

Place one cake layer on a platter or cake stand. Top with ¼ of frosting, spreading almost to edges.

Place a second cake layer on top, then spread ¼ of frosting on that layer. Top with third cake layer.

Frost cake with remaining frosting. Cover generously with shredded coconut.

ACKNOWLEDGMENTS

We owe our ongoing success to the entire 4Rivers Smokehouse team. These good people are the heart and soul of our restaurants. Without them, this book never would have happened.

Jonathan Albers
Lewis Albright
Oisa Aldridge
Amber Almestica
Keith Anderson
Mariah Anderson
Tavares Annon
Kayla Assalone
Shawn Atwell
Melissa Austin
Frank Ayers
Jacob Babington
Chelsea Bacon
Philip Bartell
Shoshanah Beates
Ari Ben-Zeev
Sara Bennett
Millie Blau
Mitchell Bomotano
Kate Bosse
Mohamed Bouidre
Martha Burn
Jake Brannigan
Robin Bressler
Melanie Burdick
Justine Burdick
Ashley Calhoun
Harrison Calvert
Ashley Candelario
Juanita Carbajol
Kyle Carlson
Brian Carlson
Melani Carrig
John, Jen, Kendall, Ann & Sydney Casebier

Max Castrillon
Tyler Cate
Kelli Cavanaugh
Heather Chalkley
Ian Chance
George Chavez
Lanie Childs
Katherine Clawson
Elise Clyburn
Isaiah Coe
Marie Colon
Marisa Colucci
Alex Confer
Steven Conrado
Jose Cortes
Christina Cortes
Tasia Cortes
Hannah Cory
Jennifer Couch
Alex Crawford
Dylan Crawford
Cathryn Currie
Jim Daniel
Jessica Dasher
Mary Daughtry
Brian Davis
Jimmie Davis
Joseph Davis
Will Davis
Sallie Denson
Michael, Jo-Jo, Sarah & Daniel Dey
Bianca Diana
Leah Dieter
Claire Dixon-Valdes

Eduardo Dominguez
Douglas Doudney
Trent Duncan
Steven Dungey
Ryan Dunn
Steven Dunn
Adil Echcheikh
Bryce Echelson
Howard Edwards
Malcolm Edwards
Kamal Elyazidi
Bethany Emerson
Casey Erskine
Amanda Eubanks
Tyler Evans
Dominique Evans
Natalie Faircloth
Cecilia Farner
Jacob Fay
Jordan Fellenger
Eric Fenech
Hillary Fields
Allison Fields
Tom, Debbie, Kelsey & Matt Finn
David Flores
Kayla Forster
Terrell Francis
Marie Franck
James Frank
Alan Fuller
Dawson Furrer
Samson Fuscien
Rachael Gahagan
Samantha Gainey

Matt Galecki
Kristin Galicz
Matthew Galicz
Griselda Gamez
Morgan Gehris
Caleb George
Kayla Gibson
Nathalie Goddard
Jaycius Golding
Eugene Goss
Stephanie Gutierrez
Chad Guyot
Hugo Hall
Dillon Hallahan
Kaley Hamilton
David Hancock
John Harrer
Jolene Harris
John Hart
Robert Hellweg Jr
Andrea Henderson
Cameron Henry
Cameron Henson Jr.
Jenny Herbert
Renee Hernandez
Martin Hering
Alma Hill
Nathan Hinman
Victoria Hoa
Haley Hohnhorst
Shelcie Holbert
Tim Holcomb
Kalee Holt
Frank Hornick
Robert Horrocks

Arkee Howard
James Howard
Olivia Howard
Melissa Howe
John Hufferd
Sarah Hufferd
Alana Icenroad
Marisa Jacobson
Megan Jacques
Marianna Jaramillo
Allison Jessee
Brian Johnson
Gwen Johnston
Raymond Jones
CeCeLie Jones
Ashley Jones
Robin Joyce
Emily Justice
Joy Justice
Alexander Karimipour
Chelsea Keller
Kevin Keller
Dave Killingsworth
Christian King
Brigid Kish
David Klein
Alexis Knapp
Brooke Kobylinski
Lauren Kosiewski
Justin Lee
Rachel Leemis
Jennifer Liszcz
Emily Logan
Michael Lombardo
Amanda Lombardo
Bill Lowman
Christina Lugo
Senny Luu
Alurra MacWithey
Tarah Macwithey
Sidney Macwithey
C. Major
Myriam Manigat

Keilani Manalili
Justin Mang
Meghan Marc
Andrea Marquinez-Wulff
Samantha Martini
Bethany Mayhew
Wayne McAlpine
Sean McCall
Devon McDonough
Michael McDowell
Carolyn McDowell
Joseph McGee
Mack McMillan
Sheryl Meehan
Sarah Mendoza
Alyssa Merwin
Rebekah Mills
Dail Mills
Zach Mills
Scott Millson
Matthew Mines
Staci Moellman
Sarah Moellman
Ian Montgomery
Samuel Moore
Melissa Moore
Autre Morgan
Ralph Mosby
Miranda Mundo
Joseph Negron
Mabel Nieves
Teresa Nolan
David Nolan
Zac Norris
Michael & Kitty O'Grody
Nathaniel Orozco
Jeff & Meredith Palermo
Courtney Paster
Patricia Patterson
William Peacock
Marissa Peery
Jo-Ann Perfido
Ashley Petersen

Wesley Pinney
Bailee Polk
Chad Poore
Edward Proechel
Gertha Prudent
Helena Pumphrey
Eric Py
Kadie Quiles
John Radcliff & family
Nana Rahaim
Cody Ramos
Thomas Rayburn
Patrick Reed
Katie Rehm
Corey Reinke
Samantha Reinneck
Chris Richards
John Riley
Mema Rivers
Victoria Robinson
Jonathan Rodriguez
Tabitha Rogan
Juan Roman
Chloe Ruiz
Parker Runion
Justin Schlosser
Melinda Schmidt
Cindy Schooler
Khiana Scott
Eric, Toni, Abby
& Matt Scott
Christina Sears
Shawn Seaver
Joshua Shackelford
Brian Shackelford
Rachel Sharp
Sean Sheaf
Eric Sheen
Cassandra Shriner
Jason Silver
Cara Smith
Dillon Smith
Jason Smith

Austin Smith
Tianna Sofran
Marco Solano
Kirk Solberg
Brittany Solomon
Alexandra Speight
Melissa Spilman
Troy Staten
Dana Staten
Adam Stone
Sarah Sullivan
Rachel Terry
Colby Texeira
Elizabeth Tillman
Lauren Travers
Rick, Julie, Trip
& Katie Tressler
Victoria Van Pelt
Alexander Vance
Kayla Vazquez
Ariana Vazquez
Jason Vermeulen
James Vernace
Ashlie Vernon
James Vincent
Brian Von Dohlen
Rand & Allison Wallace
Steve Waln
Kara Walters
Brad Watkins
Jade Watts
Joe Webber
Darren Werner
Aubrey White
Lindsey White
George Wilder
Rachel Williams
Erica Williams
Tiffany Williams
Savanna Willis
Brian Wilson
Michael Yamauchi
Gregg Zuckerman

INDEX

Numbers in **bold** indicate pages with illustrations

Avocados
    Guacamole, 145–46

Bacon
    Bacon- and Spinach-Stuffed Ribeye Roast, 126–27
    Bacon and Spinach Stuffed Ribeye Roast, **127**
    Bacon-Wrapped Smoked Jalapeños, **44**, 45
    Cowboy Skillet Scramble, 90–91, **91**
    Double Chocolate Bread Pudding with Bacon- and-Hickory-Chip-Infused Crème Anglaise, 214–15, **215**

Barbecue
    heat sources, 20–21, 118–19
    origins of, 11, 20
    regional traditions, 11, 12, 14, 16, 24, 116–17

Barbecue Ministry, 14–16, 16

Beef
    Bacon- and Spinach-Stuffed Ribeye Roast, 126–27, **127**
    BBQ Quesadilla, 46, **47**
    Beef Short Ribs with Red Wine Reduction Sauce and Collard-Infused Cheese Grits, 148–49
    Big Dog Chili, 66–67
    Brisket and Cheese Grits Shepherd's Pie, 134–36, **135**
    Brisket Bruschetta, 48, **49**
    Carne Asada Nachos, **32**, 33
    Chicken-Fried Steak, 122–23, **123**
    Coffee-Crusted Cowboy Ribeye Steak, **130**, 131–32
    Grilled Brisket, Asiago, and Jalapeño Pizza, 36–37, **37**
    Longhorn Sandwich, **98**, 99
    Martha's Brunswick Stew, 72, **73**
    Oxtail Beef Stew, 128–29, **129**
    Santa Maria Tri-Tip, **124**, 125
    Smoked Brisket, 116–121, **116**, **121**
    St. Paddy's Day Brisket Burger, 104–5, **105**
    Street Tacos, 138–39, **139**
    Tequila-Spiked Steak Fajitas, **144**, 145–46
    Texas Destroyer, 106, **107**

Biscuits
    Gruyère Herb Biscuits, 88–89, **89**

Bologna
    Phoney Baloney, **110**, 111

Brussels sprouts
    Prosciutto Brussels Sprouts, 196, **196**

Cabbage
    Southern Coleslaw, 57

Cakes
    Caramel Pecan Cake, 212–13, **213**
    Coconut Cake, **216**, 217
    Red Velvet Cake, 200, **201**

Cheese
    Baked Cheese Grits, 70
    Collard-Infused Baked Cheese Grits, 71
    Grilled Ham Mac and Cheese, 96, **97**
    Hickory-Smoked, Rioja-Infused Manchego Croquettes, 42–43, **43**
    Tequila-Spiked Queso Fundido con Chorizo, 50–51, **51**

Chicken
    BBQ Quesadilla, 46, **47**
    Buttermilk Fried Chicken, 176, **177**

Martha's Brunswick Stew, 72, **73**
Smoked Chicken, 186–87, **186**
Smoked Chicken and Sausage Gumbo, 54–56, **55**
Smoked Chicken Potpie with Cheddar Buttermilk Biscones, **180–82**, 183–84
Smoked Chicken Wings, 28, **29**
Stacked Chicken Enchiladas Verde, 188–89, **189**
Street Tacos, 138–39, **139**
Chocolate
Chocolate Awesomeness, **208**, 210
Double Chocolate Bread Pudding with Bacon-and-Hickory-Chip-Infused Crème Anglaise, 214–15, **215**
Coconut
Coconut Cake, **216**, 217
Coconut Cream Pie, **202**, 203
Coffee
Coffee-Crusted Cowboy Ribeye Steak, **130**, 131–32
Coffee Rub, **22**, 131–32
Collard greens
Beef Short Ribs with Red Wine Reduction Sauce and Collard-Infused Cheese Grits, 148–49
Collard Greens with Ham, **58**, 59
Collard-Infused Baked Cheese Grits, 71
Corn
Smokehouse Corn, **62**, 63
Cornbread
Cornbread Salad, 60, **61**
Skillet Cornbread, **80**, 81
Cowboy culture, 11–12

Deen, Paula, 70, **71**, 207
Desserts
Banana Dream Pudding Cups, **209**, 211
Bourbon Pecan Pie, 204, **205**
Caramel Pecan Cake, 212–13, **213**
Chocolate Awesomeness, **208**, 210
Coconut Cake, **216**, 217
Coconut Cream Pie, **202**, 203
Double Chocolate Bread Pudding with Bacon-and-Hickory-Chip-Infused Crème Anglaise, 214–15, **215**
Krispy Kreme Bread Pudding, **206**, 207
Peanut Butter Fluff Pudding Cups, **208–9**, 210–11
Red Velvet Cake, 200, **201**
Dressing
Eric's Sausage Dressing, 197
Eggs
Cowboy Skillet Scramble, 90–91, **91**
Migas Breakfast Tortillas, 92–93, **93**
Fish
Smoked Salmon, **178**, 179
Frito Chili Pie, 67, **67**

Green beans
Southern Green Beans, 194, **194**
Grits
Baked Cheese Grits, 70
Brisket and Cheese Grits Shepherd's Pie, 134–36, **135**
Cheese Grits, 134–36
Collard-Infused Baked Cheese Grits, 71
Shrimp and Grits, 76–78, **77**
Guacamole, 145–46

Ham
Collard Greens with Ham, **58**, 59
Grilled Cuban Sandwich, 100–101, **101**
Grilled Ham Mac and Cheese, 96, **97**
Southern Green Beans, 194, **194**

Jalapeños
Bacon-Wrapped Smoked Jalapeños, **44**, 45
Grilled Brisket, Asiago, and Jalapeño Pizza, 36–37, **37**
Mustard Relish, 111
Sausage, Cheese and Jalapeño Kolaches, 84–86
James Beard House, **13**, **17**, 112

Kolaches
Fruit and Cream Cheese, 84–85, **85**

Sausage, Cheese and Jalapeño, 86

Lamb
    Braised Lamb Shanks, 160–62, **161**
    Smoked Leg of Lamb, **168**, 169
Lampe, Ray, 185, **185**
Lilly, Chris, 152, **153**

Mangos
    Diablo Shrimp with Fried Green Tomatoes and Mango Salsa, 38–40, **39**

Okra
    Fried Okra, **55**, 56
Olives
    Smoked Olives, 42–43, **43**

Palermo, Jeff, **13**, **41**, 50, 54, 63, 108
Pecans
    Bourbon Pecan Pie, 204, **205**
    Caramel Pecan Cake, 212–13, **213**
Pico de Gallo, 33, 188
Pies
    Bourbon Pecan Pie, 204, **205**
    Coconut Cream Pie, **202**, 203
Pizza
    Grilled Brisket, Asiago, and Jalapeño Pizza, 36–37, **37**
Pork
    BBQ Quesadilla, 46, **47**
    Breaded Porklette with Chipotle Aioli, 112–13, **113**
    Cochon de Lait, 108, **109**
    Cowboy Pork Chops with Soy-Honey Glaze, 170–72, **171**
    Grilled Cuban Sandwich, 100–101, **101**
    Grilled Teriyaki Pork Tenderloin with Plum Sauce, **158**, 159
    Messy Pig, **102**, 103
    Pulled Pork, 152–57, **154–55**
    Six Shooter, **30**, 31
    St. Louis Ribs, 164–65, **165**
    Street Tacos, 138–39, **139**

Potatoes
    Baked Gruyère Mashed Potatoes, 195
    Brisket and Cheese Grits Shepherd's Pie, 134–36, **135**
    Cilantro Potato Salad, **68**, 69

Rivers, John
    barbecue background of, 12, 14, 16
    Barbecue Ministry, 14–16, 16
    birth of 4Rivers Smokehouse, 14–16, **14**, **15**, **17**
    business, 12
    early life and family of, 11–12
Rubs
    4R Brisket Rub, 118
    All-Purpose Rub, **22**, 25, 156
    Brisket Rub, **23**, 25
    Coffee Rub, **22**, 131–32

Salads
    Cornbread Salad, 60, **61**
    Southern Coleslaw, 57
Salsa
    Mango Salsa, 38–40, **39**
    Pico de Gallo, 33, 188
    Salsa Verde, 188–89
Sánchez, Aarón, 50, **50**
Sandwiches
    Breaded Porklette with Chipotle Aioli, 112–13, **113**
    Cochon de Lait, 108, **109**
    Grilled Cuban Sandwich, 100–101, **101**
    Grilled Ham Mac and Cheese, 96, **97**
    Longhorn Sandwich, **98**, 99
    Messy Pig, **102**, 103
    Phoney Baloney, **110**, 111
    St. Paddy's Day Brisket Burger, 104–5, **105**
    Texas Destroyer, 106, **107**
Sauces
    All-Purpose BBQ Sauce, 25
    Bourbon Glaze, 192–93
    Brisket Burger Sauce, **22**, 104
    Chimichurri Sauce, **22**, **124**, 125
    Chipotle Aiolo, 112

Cranberry Chili Dipping Sauce, 185
Gravy, 122–23
Guasacaca Sauce, 138–39
Habanero Sauce, 138–39
Mojo Sauce, **23**, 100
Mustard BBQ Sauce, **22**, 24
Mustard Relish, 111
Pulled Pork Finishing Sauce, **23**, 157
Pulled Pork Mustard Slather, **23**, **154**, 156
regional traditions, 24
Roasted Garlic Honey Vinaigrette, 42–43
See also Salsa

Sausage
Big Dog Chili, 66–67
Cowboy Skillet Scramble, 90–91, **91**
Eric's Sausage Dressing, 197
Longhorn Sandwich, **98**, 99
Martha's Brunswick Stew, 72, **73**
Sausage, Cheese and Jalapeño Kolaches, 84–86
Smoked Chicken and Sausage Gumbo, 54–56, **55**
Tequila-Spiked Queso Fundido con Chorizo, 50–51, **51**

Scallops
Bacon-Wrapped Scallops with Cranberry Chili Dipping Sauce, 185

Shrimp
Diablo Shrimp with Fried Green Tomatoes and Mango Salsa, 38–40, **39**
Shrimp and Grits, 76–78, **77**

Soups, stews, and chili
Big Dog Chili, 66–67
Frito Chili Pie, 67, **67**
Martha's Brunswick Stew, 72, **73**
Oxtail Beef Stew, 128–29, **129**
Smoked Chicken and Sausage Gumbo, 54–56, **55**

South Beach Wine & Food Festival, 50, **50**, 152, **153**, **163**, **185**
Southern culture and food traditions, 11–12

Spinach
Bacon- and Spinach-Stuffed Ribeye Roast, 126–27
Bacon and Spinach Stuffed Ribeye Roast, **127**

Starters
Bacon-Wrapped Smoked Jalapeños, **44**, 45
BBQ Quesadilla, 46, **47**
Brisket Bruschetta, 48, **49**
Carne Asada Nachos, **32**, 33
Diablo Shrimp with Fried Green Tomatoes and Mango Salsa, 38–40, **39**
Grilled Brisket, Asiago, and Jalapeño Pizza, 36–37, **37**
Hickory-Smoked, Rioja-Infused Manchego Croquettes, 42–43, **43**
Six Shooter, **30**, 31
Smoked Chicken Wings, 28, **29**
Tequila-Spiked Queso Fundido con Chorizo, 50–51, **51**

Sweet Potato Casserole, 197

Thanksgiving, 191–97

Tomatoes
Chimichurri Sauce, **22**, **124**, 125
Diablo Shrimp with Fried Green Tomatoes and Mango Salsa, 38–40, **39**
Pico de Gallo, 33, 188
Smoked Tomato Jam, 48, **49**

Tortillas
BBQ Quesadilla, 46, **47**
Carne Asada Nachos, **32**, 33
Cowboy Skillet Scramble, 90–91, **91**
Migas Breakfast Tortillas, 92–93, **93**
Stacked Chicken Enchiladas Verde, 188–89, **189**
Street Tacos, 138–39, **139**
Tequila-Spiked Steak Fajitas, **144**, 145–46

Turkey
Smoked Turkey, 192–93, **193**

Veal
Osso Bucco, **140**, 141–42

Wood, 20–21, 118–19